THE MAKING OF
THE LOST WORLD
JURASSIC PARK

JODY DUNCAN

BALLANTINE BOOKS • NEW YORK

Copyright © 1997 MCA Publishing Rights, a Division of Universal Studios, Inc. All Rights Reserved. THE LOST WORLD: JURASSIC PARK™ & © 1997 Universal City Studios, Inc., and Amblin Entertainment, Inc. All Rights Reserved.

All rights reserved under International and Pan-American Copyright Conventions. Published in the United States by Ballantine Books, a division of Random House, Inc., New York, and simultaneously in Canada by Random House of Canada Limited, Toronto.

http://www.randomhouse.com

Library of Congress Catalog Card Number: 97-93563

ISBN: 0-345-40734-2

Interior design by Michaelis/Carpelis Design Associates, Inc.

Artwork courtesy of:	Photography by:
Stan Winston Studios	Sean Casey
Industrial Light & Magic	Peter Iovino
Greg Aronowitz	Robert Isenberg
John Bell	Paul Mejias
Matt Codd	Chuck Zlotnick
Stephan Dechant	
Sean Hargreaves	Special thanks to
George Hull	David James, unit
David Lowery	photographer, and
Todd Marks	Bette Einbinder,
Warren Manser	photo editor,
Mark "Crash" McCreery	Universal Pictures.
Joey Orosco	
Rion Vernon	

Manufactured in the United States of America

First Edition: June 1997

10 9 8 7 6 5 4 3 2 1

ACKNOWLEDGMENTS

The following pages would be barren were it not for the kindness and generosity of Steven Spielberg, Kathy Kennedy, Jerry Molen, Colin Wilson, Dave Lowery, Rick Carter, Dennis Muren, Stan Winston, Michael Lantieri, Bonnie Curtis, Jeff Goldblum, Julianne Moore, and Don Levy—gatherers, all.

A special nod goes to Jerry Schmitz, who made things happen and was always a mere phone call away.

Thanks to Nancy Cushing-Jones and Cindy Chang for their support. And, finally, big thank-yous to seven-year-old Liam Odien for use of his extensive paleontology library, and to my nine-year-old daughter, Caitlin Shannon, for all the smiles and pats on the back.

—*Jody Duncan*

Contents

Introduction

There was something similar about the three men sitting at the restaurant table that early summer afternoon, a shared quality of enthusiasm and almost boyish delight as they brainstormed and huddled over sketches quickly drawn on pieces of scratch paper. One looked slightly older than the other two, his longish, unruly hair exhibiting nearly as much salt as pepper—yet much of the electric energy at the table was emanating from him, and he was clearly the subject of the glances and shy smiles coming from the other diners.

It was June 1995, and Steven Spielberg had come to Century City's Dive!—a submarine-themed restaurant co-owned by the director himself—to discuss ideas and images for a new project with production designer Rick Carter and illustrator Dave Lowery. Their subject: *The Lost World*, the sequel to Spielberg's *Jurassic Park*.

Based on a novel by Michael Crichton, *Jurassic Park* had exploded onto movie screens in May of 1993, and proceeded to do record-breaking, mind-boggling business at the box office. Its opening weekend alone had raked in an unprecedented $50 million; and before it was done, the domestic take would multiply to seven times that amount. When added to foreign market sales, the total would reach nearly $1 billion—a figure that didn't take into account the revenue ultimately generated by home video sales and lucrative cable, television, and merchandising deals.

The movie's success could be measured in more than commercial terms, however. Recounting events on a Costa Rican island inhabited by genetically engineered dinosaurs, *Jurassic Park* had single-handedly incited a worldwide dinosaur craze. Suddenly, attendance was up at natural history museums, and television programming was flooded with paleontology-themed documentaries and specials.

Jurassic Park had also been significant for showcasing an emerging digital technology. The film's menagerie of three-dimensional, computer animated dinosaurs—which looked for all the world like living, breathing animals—were not the *first* computer generated characters to hit the big screen, but they were certainly the most complex, the most photorealistic and the most organic. The field of visual effects—which had seen few technological advancements of this magnitude in its hundred-year history—would never be the same.

Not surprisingly, there had been unofficial talk among principal players of a sequel ever since *Jurassic Park*'s release; and those discussions intensified when Michael Crichton completed the manuscript for his follow-up novel, *The*

Director Steven Spielberg on the set of *The Lost World: Jurassic Park*.

Lost World. Soon afterward, Spielberg, Crichton, and *Jurassic Park* screenwriter David Koepp entered into a gentlemen's agreement to bring *The Lost World* to the screen, under the umbrella of Universal Pictures and Amblin Entertainment, Spielberg's production company.

The film's real conception, however, took place that June afternoon at Dive!, as Spielberg, Carter, and Lowery first began "making pictures"—a process that would continue for several months. Storyboards would not only be used to illustrate specific sequences, they would actually serve as a means of *developing* those sequences and the overall storyline. Nearly all of Spielberg's films had evolved in the same way, resulting in some of the most indelible cinematic images of the past two decades—a fleet of saucers racing around a bend in a country road in *Close Encounters of the Third Kind*; the silhouette of a bicycle against a frame-filling moon in *E.T.: The Extra-Terrestrial*; a tyrannosaurus rex roaring among the ruins of a skeletal display in *Jurassic Park*; a little girl in red against a sea of gray humanity in *Schindler's List*.

The Lost World would be as visually driven as any of those previous films. And so, before there was a script, before there was a cast or crew, before there was even a published novel, Steven Spielberg sat down with his artistic collaborators and began sketching images, working throughout the afternoon, pausing only to oblige frequent requests for an autograph.

The meeting at Dive! was followed that summer by similar sessions at Spielberg's home; then, in July, the small but seminal team went its separate ways—Carter and Lowery to complete current projects, and Spielberg to a family vacation in Greece and East Hampton. Even while vacationing, however, the director's imagination turned again and again to *The Lost World* and he continued to produce his own crude little storyboards throughout the summer, noting story ideas in the margins.

Those ideas and images would not reach their ultimate fruition for two years, when *The Lost World* had its Memorial Day 1997 opening. Like its predecessor, the movie gripped audiences from the first moments, when a curious little girl approaches what looks like a chicken-sized lizard on a Costa Rican island beach. A scream is heard. Something has survived.

Cutting to New York, we learn from an ailing John Hammond that there was a second island facility that fed his dream of Jurassic Park—a "Site B" where the grittier work of dinosaur cloning took place. In the four years since the disaster at Jurassic Park, the facility has been destroyed by a hurricane and the animals have been left to thrive on Isla Sorna—now a true lost world such as that imagined by Sir Arthur Conan Doyle. His InGen company in bankruptcy and taken over by a mercenary nephew, Hammond has only one remaining desire: to send an expedition to the site to document its Jurassic-era wildlife, thereby protecting the sanctity of the habitat and restoring his reputation as a visionary. Summoned to lead the four-person expedition is Ian Malcolm, the eccentric but brilliant mathematician who nearly lost his life on Isla Nublar four years earlier.

Upon arrival on the island, the group's benevolent intentions are soon at odds with a second expedition, sent by the faltering InGen corporation to round up the animals and return them stateside, where "Jurassic Park–San Diego" is being built as a means to restore the company's fiscal health. Within hours both camps have been destroyed, and the survivors of the two philosophically opposed expeditions must join forces against the dinosaur population. In the end, philosophies give way to a fierce, single-minded struggle for survival, both within and outside the boundaries of the lost world.

Film teasers and posters for the film began to appear nearly six months before its unveiling. Those provocative images, coupled with the four years that had passed since the release of *Jurassic Park*, whetted audience appetites for *The Lost World;* and when it was finally released, it generated all the excitement one would expect of a new *Jurassic Park* saga directed by Steven Spielberg.

The Lost World was the fourth movie to bear the title, but the first to bear the Spielberg stamp. It was the most anticipated sequel ever released. It was *the* event film of the summer. It was an adventure 65 million—and two—years in the making....

CHAPTER 1

JUNE 1995:
LOS ANGELES

The Birth of Spielberg Moments

It was summer 1995, and Steven Spielberg hadn't directed a movie in more than two years. After completing *Schindler's List*—the 1993 film that won universal critical acclaim and seven Oscars, including those for best picture and best director—Spielberg had opted to step away from the camera for a while and enjoy the personal and professional rewards the film had brought to him. He was hardly idle, however, continuing to oversee in-the-works projects at Amblin Entertainment and serving as executive producer on features such as *Casper* and *Twister*. His time had also been occupied by projects being developed under the banner of DreamWorks SKG, the new company he had recently formed with partners Jeffrey Katzenberg and David Geffen.

Throughout the hiatus, Spielberg had considered carefully what his next directing project might be. Rumors held that he was interested in a psychological thriller entitled *Blue Vision*, or that he might be up for another installment of the *Indiana Jones* saga. But what seemed to spark his imagination the most was *The Lost World*, novelist Michael Crichton's follow-up to *Jurassic Park*. Spielberg had adapted the

Opposite: Sequences for *The Lost World* were developed through hundreds of illustrations and concept paintings generated by the art department in the year preceding production. Pictured here, a concept painting by illustrator Matt Codd.
Below: A digital rendering of the Site B laboratory complex, executed in Photoshop.

Above: Illustrator Sean Hargreaves' depiction of a scene in which the hunters' base camp is destroyed by escaping dinosaurs. *Right:* Janus Kaminski, director of photography. *Below:* Stan Winston with baby T-rex.

first novel into a spectacularly successful feature, and had found the making of that film to be pure joy. Now, reading the still unpublished manuscript of *The Lost World*, he began to consider the compelling yarn a candidate for his return to directing.

Crichton's new story was set six years after the disastrous ending of *Jurassic Park,* in which scientists sent to sign off on a theme park with live dinosaurs barely escape with their lives. In *The Lost World,* one of those scientists—mathematician Ian Malcolm—learns that something has survived on a second island, Isla Sorna, Jurassic Park's behind-the-scenes "Site B." With a small group of researchers, Malcolm investigates the island, pitting himself not only against the thriving Jurassic-era inhabitants, but also the science-for-profit firms attempting to exploit them.

Intrigued by the story, Spielberg negotiated a deal with Universal Pictures and began to pull together a creative team, nearly every member of which was a veteran of *Jurassic Park*. Serving with Spielberg as executive producer was Kathleen Kennedy, a co-founder and onetime president of Amblin who had since formed her own production company, Kennedy/Marshall. Producers Jerry Molen and Colin Wilson would also return to the fold, along with *Jurassic Park* screenwriter David Koepp.

Another returning department head was production designer Rick Carter, a veteran not only of the original film, but of blockbusters such as *Back to the Future II* and *III* and *Forrest Gump*. Visual effects supervisor Dennis Muren, creature effects supervisor Stan Winston, and special effects supervisor Michael Lantieri—the effects triad that had combined talents to create the dinosaur effects for *Jurassic Park*—also committed to the sequel. Of all the department heads, only director of photography Janusz Kaminski—who had shot *Schindler's List* for Spielberg—was not an alumnus of *Jurassic Park*.

Ironically, the most essential role—that of director—remained unfilled, since, at this early stage, Spielberg had not yet decided whether he would direct the movie. But that fact did not at all dampen his enthusiasm for the project. All summer long, Spielberg had been cranking out sketches and ideas for the film; upon his return to his offices at Amblin/DreamWorks, he turned them over to Rick Carter and Dave Lowery, who would spend the next several months translating the rough, seminal images into refined storyboards. "They were funny little drawings," Lowery noted, "but they were accurate compositionally, in that they had a foreground, middle ground, and background. And they showed, fairly well, the staging he was thinking of for particular shots. It was fun to get these drawings because, through them, he came up with some wonderful 'Spielberg shots.' I loved being in on the birth of those Spielberg moments."

The lab complex—with a parasaurolophus herd in the foreground—as envisioned by the art department. The lab evolved through a variety of designs before a final look was established.

Right: Production designer
Rick Carter.

A small notation Spielberg had made in
the margin of one of his sketches read:
"This is a story of hunters and gatherers."
The passing thought would become the
seed from which the entire movie grew.
"At the time," Rick Carter commented,
"he was only referring to one particular
sequence. But the idea of hunters and

Above and right: Producing
designs for an abandoned
worker village—a key set-
ting in Michael Crichton's
novel—accounted for much
of the art department's
early activity. The village is
rendered in ink and water-
color.

gatherers came to be the basis of the whole movie. There would be two groups coming to the island, hunters and gatherers, and those groups would be encountering hunters and gatherers in the dinosaur realm. Ultimately, the story became one about the battle between these species for position at the top of the food chain. Everything we came up with for this movie extended out of that one idea."

Although it would be based solidly on Crichton's novel, the film's story would take its own shape as it moved through the storyboarding process—just as the visualizations for *Jurassic Park* had cemented that film's storyline. "One of the reasons *Jurassic Park* did as well in foreign markets as it did here," Carter proposed, "was that it was such a visual story, it was able to cross all language barriers. That was particularly amazing since, literally, the first sixty minutes of that movie is a seminar on paleontology and genetics, cloning, how the park functions, how the park security system functions, how the computers are programmed, chaos theory. Learning about all of those subjects is just about the only thing that hap-

pens in the first half of the movie. It becomes almost funny; and finally, Malcolm acknowledges it and says, 'Uh, there *are* going to be dinosaurs on this tour, aren't there?' And we laugh, in part because we're thinking the same thing by then—'Uh, there *are* going to be dinosaurs in this dinosaur movie, aren't there?' It was necessary, but it set up tremendous expectations for the second half of the movie—because if the movie didn't deliver after making everyone wait sixty minutes, it would have been a disas-

Above: Developing story sequences were translated into ink storyboards by David Lowery. Storyboarding commenced in Fall 1995 and continued until the start of principal photography.
Left: Another early rendering of the worker village.

ter. But it did deliver; and it delivered almost entirely through the visual. The whole second half of *Jurassic Park* is one long visualization."

In the first sequence to be story-boarded from Crichton's novel *The Lost World,* a male and a female tyrannosaurus rex go in search of their baby. Finding the infant in the hands of Malcolm and Sarah—the latter a field biologist who has taken the baby T-rex to a trailer laboratory to set its broken leg—the T-rexes erupt into a protective rage, attacking the trailer and pushing it over the edge of a cliff. The "T-rex-versus-the-trailer" scene was a centerpiece of Crichton's book, and Spielberg envisioned it as a prominent scene in the movie as well.

As summer rolled on, Lowery continued to render storyboards for this and other sequences, while Carter began conceptualizing environments in which the film's action would be set. Rather than

Below: Specific areas of the town were reproduced in larger scale.

render the concept art entirely in ink or paint, Carter used computer programs such as Photoshop to mix and match a variety of photographs and paintings, creating entirely new locales. "Rick used to do a lot of work with collages to put together images," Lowery stated. "Now, he uses Photoshop in a very similar way. It is a great medium for him, because it easily accommodates the way he likes to work. When Steven saw some of these computer paintings, he said, 'This is great! Where is this place?' And Rick said, 'It doesn't exist. I made it up.'"

Among Carter's early computer-produced images were concepts for an abandoned worker village featured in the novel. According to Crichton's narrative, the town had once housed InGen's secret team of genetic scientists and was the site of a behind-the-scenes laboratory where experiments and cloning attempts—not suited for public exhibition—were conducted. "I didn't know, at this point, where the abandoned town might fit into the movie," Carter noted, "but I thought it would probably be an important place, so I started doing concepts. I found pictures of an island village that we used as the basis for the abandoned town. Then we came up with ideas for making it look very overgrown, as if the jungle was reclaiming it. In this movie, you would be seeing a world that was returning to nature—more primordial and more conducive to the dinosaurs' way of life than to ours."

By August, Carter's 2-D concepts for the town had taken more definite shape, and model maker Greg Aronowitz was hired to convert those images into a three-dimensional miniature. "Except for Rick Carter and David Lowery," Aronowitz observed, "I was the first art department person hired for *The Lost World*—and that will be my best story when I'm old and I talk about my career. Things were still very ambiguous at the time, so Rick thought it would be a good idea to present Steven Spielberg with a three-dimensional model, something that would be more clear than sketches or storyboards." By the time Aronowitz came on, Spielberg had established that the film's finale would include a scene in which the leading characters are chased through the abandoned town by velociraptors—but the action beats of that chase had yet to be determined. "The action wasn't nailed down any more than just, 'There's a chase in this town,' " Aronowitz said. "By building the town in three dimensions, Steven would have something to look at and move his eye through, as if moving his camera. All the possible scenarios for the chase could be worked out in this three-dimensional space."

Left and below: To enable Spielberg to choreograph a climactic raptor chase within the village, two-dimensional renderings were translated into a one-thirty-fifth scale tabletop miniature by model maker Greg Aronowitz. The model of the hurricane-damaged town was detailed with scaled set dressing such as miniature trees, vehicles, dinosaurs, and human figures.

Spielberg, producer Jerry Molen, and Stan Winston confer with paleontologist Jack Horner (second from left) who served as a consultant on the film.

Arriving for his first day of work on a Monday, Aronowitz constructed a rough version of the 1/35th scale miniature in time for a Thursday presentation to Spielberg. The completed model not only included town buildings, but also set dressing pieces such as model Jeeps and dinosaurs to create a clearer sense of scale. When Spielberg arrived at the art department annex for the presentation, the entire town was laid out before him on a tabletop. "He saw this miniature," Aronowitz recalled, "took a step back and said, 'Whoa! A toy!' And then he dove right into it, planning camera angles and action sequences right then and there. It proved what Rick Carter had been saying—that to design in 3-D was a real improvement over two-dimensional pictures."

"Steven was able to use what we had designed for the town to construct the scene that takes place there," Carter added. "It was a great way to do it, from my point of view, because it meant that we got to influence what would actually happen in the movie. The sequence came *out of* the environment, in a sense. That is unusual; but it's one of the joys of work-

ing with Steven on this kind of movie."

While the art department continued its production of illustrations and concepts, Spielberg engaged the Stan Winston Studio to begin work on designs for the movie's dinosaurs. A multiple Academy Award winner, Winston and his crew had been instrumental in the success of *Jurassic Park*, not only designing the creatures, but also building and puppeteering full-size animatronic raptors, an ailing triceratops, a spitting dilophosaur, and a full-size, hydraulically driven T-rex. The studio had been an equally important contributor to other high-profile effects films—such as the two *Terminator* and *Predator* films—but without question *Jurassic Park* was the biggest, most complex project in its ten-year history.

The studio's assignment for *The Lost World* would be even more ambitious, a surprise considering that some—including Winston himself—had wondered if animatronic dinosaurs would be featured in the sequel at all. *Jurassic Park* had broken ground with animated characters generated entirely through sophisticated, high-end computer graphics by Industrial Light & Magic. The creation of those computer generated (CG) dinosaurs had been a painful and laborious two-year effort; but now, three years later, the learning curve had arced and CG characters of greater or lesser complexity were becoming increasingly common in both movies and television commercials. In fact, as *The Lost World* entered its development phase, CG polar bears were selling cola in television ads, the creators of *The Simpsons* were planning an episode featuring a three-dimensional, computer generated Homer, and the first all-computer-animated feature, *Toy Story*, was about to be released. ILM itself was just

coming off a huge CG assignment for *Jumanji* and was currently computer-animating the dragon for the 1996 theatrical release, *Dragonheart*.

The mix and matching of ILM's computer animation with Winston's live-action dinosaurs had worked to great effect in the first film. But with improved digital technology at his disposal, some had predicted that Spielberg would dispense with animatronics altogether for the sequel, opting to computer generate all of *The Lost World*'s dinosaurs. "I was very concerned that Steven would go all CG with *The Lost World*," Stan Winston admitted. "My thinking is that you have to create characters first and foremost; and then you use whatever technology is best suited to creating the most realistic illusion. I am a huge fan of CG and I realize what an incredible tool it is in creating characters for film—but I don't believe in technology leading the creative process. If you can do it live, do it live."

Shortly after initiating the *Lost World*

Left: Artist renderings of the raptor chase through the workers' village. *Below:* An early artist rendering by the Stan Winston Studios.

project, Spielberg informed Winston of his intention to create the movie's dinosaurs in the same way he had for *Jurassic Park*—by artfully intercutting the mechanical versions with computer animated characters, using the latter for shots requiring multiple creatures or more dynamic, full-body action. "Steven wanted to feature some dinosaur characters that were primarily practical," Colin Wilson said. "I think he felt that there is a

rapport and intimacy that develops with the animals when they are right there on the set—something that is difficult to achieve when the actors are working against nothing but air or a measuring pole."

The execution of the computer generated dinosaurs would again be assigned to

Because of popular demand, Spielberg and the production team were adamant that a stegosaurus be featured in this movie. Here are early renderings from the Stan Winston Studios of the baby and adult stegosaurus.

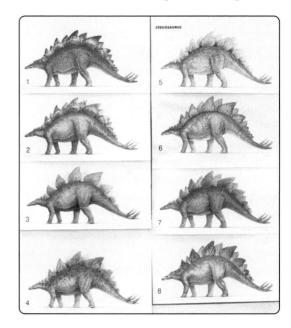

visual effects supervisor Dennis Muren and a team of artisans at Industrial Light & Magic. A veteran of George Lucas's *Star Wars* trilogy and a key member of the seminal ILM effects team, Muren had contributed his visual effects artistry to films such as *Close Encounters of the Third Kind, Indiana Jones and the Temple of Doom, The Abyss, Terminator 2, Jurassic Park,* and *Casper,* earning eight Academy Awards in the process.

Muren and the digital pioneers at ILM had won well-deserved kudos for their ground-breaking work on the first film, an effort akin to NASA's Apollo program in its intensity and single-mindedness of purpose—albeit on a smaller scale. "When we took on *Jurassic Park,*" Muren noted, "we didn't even know if we *could* do it; and, as a result, we didn't go into that show confidently or boldly. Going into *The Lost World,* we knew what was possible, and we were eager to test the limits of the technology and take it to a new level. Phil Tippett, the animation director for *Jurassic Park,* had an expression: 'We built the Stradivarius, and now we're learning to play it.' That was the way I felt toward *The Lost World*—we had built the means for doing it in the first show, and now we were going to have the opportunity to play music with it."

With both the live-action and CG effects creators on board, Spielberg began to zero in on the dinosaur species that would be featured in the new movie. Early determination was crucial, since a long lead time would be necessary for the design of those dinosaurs by the Stan Winston Studio, and their ultimate construction in both the physical and virtual realms. "We took storyboards that Steven had laid out," recalled Colin Wilson, who would interface with the animatronic and CG teams directly, "and chose the species that would be represented from those boards. Steven had already done some research, and he'd spoken to our paleontology consultant, Jack Horner, about what kind of dinosaurs he wanted to see this time." Spielberg had also taken public response into account. After having received literally thousands of letters—many from children—inquiring as to why there had been no stegosaurs in *Jurassic Park,* he was adamant that the huge, plated dinosaur would be featured in the new movie. "Steven made that his mission—to come up with a really good stegosaurus sequence."

In addition to the stegosaurus, other dinosaurs on the 'must-have' list included the T-rex and raptors, the predators responsible for the first movie's most intense, suspenseful sequences. But until the story was more thoroughly hashed out and a definitive script delivered—something that in the late summer of '95 was still months away—there remained questions as to what other dinosaurs would populate Spielberg's lost world. "As we started implementing the design work for *The Lost World,*" Stan Winston recalled, "we knew we were going to bring the T-rex back—a male, a female, *and* a baby—and that there would be raptors in a big chase at the end of the movie. The T-rexes, the raptors, and the stegosaurus were the only absolutes at this point. The only other thing we knew for sure was that we would be designing and building a whole slew of dinosaurs that hadn't been seen in the first movie."

As summer turned to fall, Winston and the dinosaur design team set themselves to the task.

CHAPTER 2

**SEPTEMBER 1995
LOS ANGELES**

Moving Forward

While following develop-ments at the Stan Winston Studio, Industrial Light & Magic, and the art department at Amblin, Spielberg entered into early brainstorming sessions with David Koepp, the screenwriter who had scripted *Jurassic Park*. "We didn't go into *Jurassic Park* assuming that there would be a sequel," Koepp recalled. "But when the movie came out and it was such a big success and people warmed to it so wonderfully, we naturally started to talk about it. We realized that this arena pre-sented a lot of opportunities for great sto-ries. Crichton's original novel and the movie that followed had done something extraordinary—they made people sus-pend their mountain of disbelief that an island with living dinosaurs could exist in present day. That was, without doubt, the most difficult element of this whole saga. But all of that heavy lifting had already been done. So if we wanted to do a sequel, that premise was all set up and out there. Michael Crichton expressed interest in writing another novel. Steven expressed interest in doing the sequel. And my atti-tude was, 'If you guys are in, I'm in.'"

Two years passed, during which Koepp wrote and developed the project that would mark his feature film directing debut, *The Trigger Effect*. When principal photography on *The Trigger Effect* wrapped in September, the screenwriter began drafting *The Lost World* script, even as he labored at an editing suite to com-plete his own film. "The script came together in a couple of different ways," Koepp explained. "Sometimes Steven would dream up a sequence and story-board it, and then I would incorporate it into the script. Other times, I would write a sequence first; and if Steven liked it, it would be storyboarded. The ideas went back and forth between what I was writ-ing and what Steven was doing through the storyboards. My primary challenge—in both of these movies—was to find the

Opposite: The Stan Winston Studio designed all of the dinosaurs, in addition to building full-size mechani-cal characters. A sketch of the pachycephalosaurus by Winston Studio concept art director Crash McCreery. *Below:* Spielberg and Winston examine a scaled sculpture of the stegosaurus.

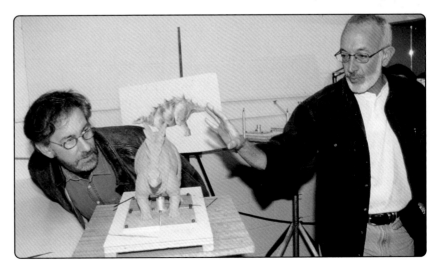

Spielberg and screenwriter David Koepp.

structure and the characters that would support the adventure. The great thing was that I had a long time to work on this script—a year from the time I started writing to the time we started shooting."

Koepp initiated the year-long writing project by reading Crichton's novel four times, highlighting characters and sequences he found particularly compelling. "If I highlighted the same sequence all four times I read it, I knew it was something wonderful and that it should be in the movie," Koepp said. A "something wonderful" that jumped out at Koepp—just as it had Spielberg— was Crichton's T-rex-versus-the-trailer sequence. "I thought that sequence was brilliant suspense. It doesn't get any better than that."

While keeping an eye out for sequences that would translate well to the screen, Koepp also looked for opportunities to eliminate characters and scenes—a structural necessity of condensing the nearly 400-page novel into a coherent, two-hour movie. "The logistics of reduction alone made the writing of the script daunting," Koepp remarked. "I wanted to take the best stuff from the book, of course, while adding things of my own. It was also important to combine characters, since this was going to be an ensemble story. I wanted everybody in that ensemble to be interesting and have a specific, important function in the story. The time the audience was going to get to spend with each character was limited, so it had to be doled out carefully. In this case, we had two ensembles—the hunters and the gatherers—and that was a lot of people to keep straight in people's heads. Eliminating characters was one of the first things I tried to do."

An early fatality was Arby Benton, the

novel's genius eleven-year-old who, with thirteen-year-old schoolmate Kelly Curtis, hides in a customized trailer and finds himself in the middle of the Site B expedition. In Koepp's screenplay, Kelly would be the lone stowaway, as well as Malcolm's own daughter. "The relationship between Malcolm and Kelly became vital to the story," Koepp commented. "It was what made the story come alive for me. On one level, this story evolved into one about parenthood and the instinct to protect your young. That idea ran through the human *and* animal characters. The classic writer's rule is, 'only connect,' and this connected—the T-rex to its young, and Malcolm to his. I liked the fact that both *Jurassic Park* movies were about families. It created the sense that this movie was a descendant of the first, and that certain inherited traits had been carried on."

On a more superficial level, the story evolved into one of survival. "*Jurassic Park* was philosophical about the existence of the dinosaurs and how they came to be and how they would coexist with human beings," said Koepp. "We had thoroughly explored those questions in the first movie, so I didn't want to return to them. *The Lost World* is less philosophical and more about basic survival. We have these two groups of people, the hunters and the gatherers, and not only are they in conflict with the dinosaurs, they are in direct conflict with each other, both philosophically and physically. It was a situation that gave us a lot to write about." In writing the sequel, Koepp drew not only from *The Lost World*, but from the original *Jurassic Park* novel, reinserting scenes that had not made it into the first movie. An example was an opening scene in which a young girl is attacked by what appears to be a large lizard. "It was a terrific scene in the book that just didn't fit the story we were telling in the first movie. But it provided a wonderful opening for this movie."

While relying heavily on both the first and second novels, Koepp also crafted entirely new sequences, such as one in which the expedition party is hunted by a trio of raptors hidden in shoulder-high grass. "I'd been reading a lot of hunting literature," Koepp recalled, "and found something about jaguars in South America hunting in long grass. I told Steven about it and he said, 'Wow—there's an interesting visual.' It suggested these fields in which you can't even see the animals, only the wakes they leave as they move through the grass. In many of Steven's movies, going all the way back to *Jaws,* the scariest moments are those where you don't see the thing you're afraid of."

As Koepp labored on the script throughout the fall of 1995, the low-level buzz of activity in the small art department at Amblin became an audible hum. Dave Lowery was now on *The Lost World* full-time, drawing black-and-white storyboards as quickly as Spielberg and Koepp could furnish new ideas. Free of his previous obligations, Rick Carter began to accelerate the design of environments and sets, particularly for the abandoned worker village.

Carter also spent much of that early fall scouting locations for the film. "The day after Labor Day, I embarked on a series of location scouts," Carter recalled. "I went to Hawaii, then Puerto Rico, New Zealand, and Australia. We didn't consider going to Costa Rica or anywhere in South America because we knew we would be shooting right in the middle of their rainy season." Of all the places Carter scouted, it was New Zealand that most stirred his imagination. "I saw imagery on the South Island of New Zealand that I had never seen before. It had silver beech trees covered with moss—more like a forest than a tropical locale. New Zealand was a great place, with really exotic, unique scenery."

Carter returned from this first scout convinced that in New Zealand the production would be able to capture the look of a lost world. Practically, however, he also knew that the long-distance location would be most suitable to second-unit establishing shots and a limited main unit shoot. Another logistical consideration was that many of the forest sequences—which would feature ILM's computer generated dinosaurs—would have to be filmed at the front of the production schedule to allow enough lead time for the time-consuming CG effort. To accommodate scheduling and transportation concerns, Carter began to search for stateside locations that might stand in for New Zealand for at least some of the first unit photography.

One location that was a strong possibility in Carter's mind was Northern California's redwood forest. "I knew the redwoods had a lot of ferns and thick for-

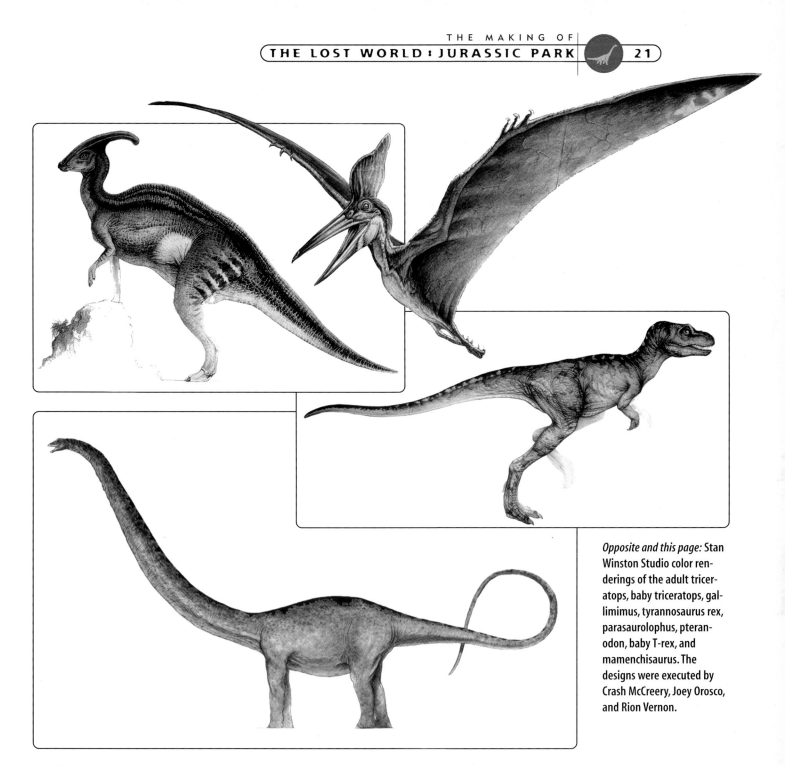

Opposite and this page: Stan Winston Studio color renderings of the adult triceratops, baby triceratops, gallimimus, tyrannosaurus rex, parasaurolophus, pteranodon, baby T-rex, and mamenchisaurus. The designs were executed by Crash McCreery, Joey Orosco, and Rion Vernon.

est," Carter explained, "and as long as the camera didn't pull back too far, I didn't think it would be recognized as the redwoods." Carter scouted the sixty-mile area between Eureka and Crescent City, located south of the Oregon border on the California coast. "What was cool about it was that, when I was in the middle of it, it *felt* like dinosaur country. The conifer was the type of environment dinosaurs really lived in, not the tropics. The idea of dinosaurs in the jungle is really an invention of the movies. So this kind of terrain was more authentic. With its huge, ancient trees, the area also offered a scale that was interesting. Finally, I liked the idea because I thought it would be an unexpected choice—audiences would be surprised to see dinosaurs in that type of environment. We knew it

Right: McCreery at work on a pencil sketch.

Because the film would feature male *and* female dinosaurs, new color schemes were devised. *Below left:* A color sketch of the male raptor. To simulate nature, the male hides were more colorful than those of the females. *Below, right and middle:* Sketches of the pachycephalosaurus. *Below, left:* The finalized pachycephalosaurus maquette. Maquettes for each character were sculpted, then painted.

was a risk because there was the chance people would say, 'What are redwoods doing off the coast of Costa Rica?' But there's something to be said for the romance of wish fulfillment—what you *want* something to be, rather than what it literally would be."

As Carter roamed the splendor of the redwood forests, dinosaur designs were being implemented at the Stan Winston Studio. After an entire summer of storyboarding, Spielberg now had a much clearer idea regarding the specific dinosaurs that would inhabit his film. The first dinosaur to make an appearance in the film would be a compsognathus—a "compy"—the small, head-bobbing creature encountered by a little girl on the Isla Sorna shore. Compys would make a return appearance later in the film, when

a large group attacks a hunter who has wandered away from the group and into the forest. A herd of stegosaurs would be featured soon after the gatherer expedition arrives on the island. In the scene, Sarah attempts to photograph and study a baby, and is attacked by the herd's alpha male when her automatic camera rewind

startles the animals. A roundup scene—in which the hunter group, equipped with snagger vehicles and high-tech weapons, maneuvers through a stampede of herbivores—would feature the ostrichlike gallimimus; the duck-billed, hollow-crested parasaurolophus; the huge mamenchisaurus; and the bony-crested pachycephalosaurus.

In addition, a male and female T-rex would be featured throughout—in the T-rex-versus-the-trailer sequence, the "rex raid" in which the animals destroy a campsite, and in the film's finale—as would their baby. Velociraptors would be seen in two major sequences, including the climactic chase through the abandoned town. Finally, a triceratops would make a brief appearance in a scene in which animals captured in the roundup are freed from their cages and proceed to create havoc at the hunter campsite. Of the nine species featured

in the film, five—the tyrannosaurus, velociraptor, gallimimus, triceratops, and parasaurolophus—had been designed and realized for *Jurassic Park*. New to the sequel were the pachycephalosaurus, compsognathus, mamenchisaurus and stegosaurus, all of which would be designed from scratch. "One of the wonderful things about *Jurassic Park*," Stan Winston remarked, "was that it allowed people to see animals they'd never seen

Top, left and below: Finalized painted maquettes of the male raptor and the baby stegosaurus. *Top, right:* A Crash McCreery sketch of a compsognathus.

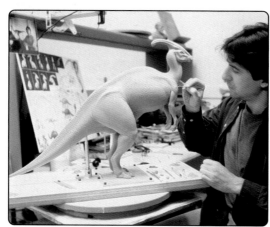

Above: Artist Bill Basso at work on the baby T-rex maquette. *Above, right:* The baby stegosaurus, sculpted by Jon Neill and Christian Lau. *Near right:* Paul Mejias details the parasaurolophus maquette. *Far right:* The pachycephalosaurus maquette was sculpted by Scott Stoddard. *Below, right:* Jason Matthews finalizes a pteranodon-head sculpture. *Below, left:* Adult stegosaurus sculpture with cut-out figure (of artist Christian Lau) to show scale.

before. We felt that it was our responsibility to do that for the audience in this movie as well—give them something new, while also bringing back some of the characters they'd be disappointed not to see again."

New characters, as well as those slated for filming early in the production sched-

ule, were given priority status. The baby T-rex and the baby and adult stegosaurs fell into both categories, and thus were among the first characters on the design agenda. Concept art director Mark "Crash" McCreery—the illustrator who had rendered initial sketches of the dinosaurs for *Jurassic Park*—became very much involved in the design phase, along with concept designers Joey Orosco and Rion Vernon. "We started designing the new dinosaurs," Winston said, "with Crash doing renderings for the pachycephalosaurus, the compy, and the adult stegosaur. Joey Orosco rendered the baby T-rex, and Rion Vernon did the initial rendering of the baby stegosaur."

From initial pencil drawings, designs moved into color renderings and maquettes—small-scaled sculptures through which the final three-dimensional forms and paint schemes would be determined. "We had to design new paint schemes not only for the new dinosaurs, but for some of the already-designed dinosaurs from the last movie," Winston explained, "because now there were male dinosaurs, as well as females; and typically in nature, the males of any species are far more brightly colored. We also wanted to make sure that the audience would be able to tell the males and females apart. It was a great deal of fun to run the gamut of color and come up with interesting designs. The colors on the females for the first film had been fairly subdued; but with male animals, there were many more possible colorations."

The Winston shop also provided designs and painted maquettes for dinosaurs that would be created in CG only, such as the mamenchisaurus—rendered by McCreery, then detailed out in color by Jim Charmatz. Those maquettes were then turned over to ILM for scanning, giving the digital team a jumping-off point for the building of the computer models. Paul Mejias sculpted and painted a parasaurolophus maquette for that purpose, as well as a second, possible sculpture that was used as reference for a full-size parasaurolophus carcass that

would be built by a crew working under Mejias and Tim Larsen.

As they had for the first film, the designers at the Winston studio adhered closely to paleontological fact—or, in the absence of fact, paleontological theory—in their dinosaur renderings and sculptures. "We were very concerned that whatever we came up with made sense scientifically," Winston said, "so we drew from the science of paleontology. But since that science is limited in detail and has to rely only on bone structure and hypothesis, we also drew from nature— what we see around us today. We looked at the color schemes and hide textures of existing animals, especially those that live in a similar environment and have a similar lifestyle to the dinosaurs. The third thing we pulled from, of course, was imagination and instinct. No one really knows what these animals looked like; but our instincts told us if what we'd come up with made sense."

Scientific accuracy was ensured for the entire production—as it had been for the first—by the commissioning of paleontologist Jack Horner to act as consultant to the film. "We took a little license from time to time in the design of the dinosaurs," Colin Wilson remarked, "but we never went too far out on a limb unless Jack Horner said it was okay. He was in and out throughout this phase, looking at all the drawings, all the sculpts, and he gave each his blessing. That was always reassuring to us. The last thing we wanted was to end up getting thousands of letters about how inaccurate our dinosaurs were."

In some cases, that commitment to accuracy strongly influenced the thrust and action of the story. While still storyboarding the original ending of the film, for example, Spielberg had toyed with the idea of having pteranodons swoop down onto both human and animal characters, carrying them off in their giant beaks. But when Jack Horner was consulted about the idea, his answer was a firm no. "Jack said that these animals were like flying stomachs," Wilson recalled, "and that they wouldn't attack something just for the sake of attacking it. So we abandoned some of those crazy ideas. Throughout the design process, Steven was very conscious of not going beyond what these animals would and could do. A very important part of the design process was making sure that the action Steven came

Digital storyboards provided more detailed renderings than those achieved by hand. Photoshop conceptual images—produced by Stefan Dechant—for an early, never realized scene within the T-rex cave. In the final film, the cave is featured in a scene in which the baby T-rex is snatched from its nest.

up with in the storyboards was actually possible, given what is known about these dinosaurs. And, when it was necessary, we went back and made revisions in the storyboards to accommodate accuracy."

Each step of a particular creature's design—from initial sketch to final painted maquette—was presented to Spielberg for approval. "Steven first signed off on the two-dimensional drawing," Winston explained, "then he signed off on a color scheme. From there, he signed off on the maquette, and finally, the painting on the maquette, which allowed him to see a small-scale version of the final character. At that point, the

Additional Photoshop renderings.

Dechant's digital concept paintings of the stegosaurus herd.

design was completed and we were free to go on to full-size sculptures."

While key artists were refining the dinosaur designs, other members of the Winston team began refurbishing existing structures, particularly those for the T-rex and raptors. None of the original animatronic characters from *Jurassic Park* had survived intact—since foam latex skins decay fairly quickly—but their underlying mechanical armatures had been carefully stored and maintained. The epoxy molds taken from the original T-rex and raptor sculptures were also in usable condition, which meant the two characters would not have to be resculpted. "A lot of the labor and cost of

these characters is in the initial designs and sculptures," Wilson noted, "but because they had already been designed, sculpted, and molded, we were able to save ourselves those costs." The head start afforded by the existing armatures and molds was a godsend; but the dinosaur construction for *The Lost World* was still an oversized, complicated assignment. "We actually had *more* to build this time, but less time to build it in," Winston commented. "For *Jurassic Park*, we started designing dinosaurs two years before filming, and we had a whole year to build them. This time, we had to design and build everything in a year."

Fall was an embryonic period for all of

already better, because Steven had been able to free up his mind, without concerning himself with the kinds of limitations the CG effects had imposed on him last time. Throughout the storyboarding process, I was always encouraging Steven to be wild with the shot designs. That was the direction I wanted to go in, in terms of our work, and I didn't want him to feel that he had to be conservative. But my energies were even more focused on how we could make the animation and the characters themselves better. That was my major concern at the beginning, and it remained my major concern for the following months."

To prepare for the show, Muren began to put together a team of modelers, animators, and technical directors. "Most of the people who had worked on the original show—people like Mark Dippé and Steve Williams—had gone on to become supervisors and directors, and weren't available to do *The Lost World*," Muren said. "After the success of *Jurassic Park*, that had become a very prized team of people; and so, naturally, they moved on. The other problem was that this show was bigger than the last one, and we were going to have to do it in a shorter length of time. Just finding the number of people we would need and the kind of talent we would need was a big deal."

The determination of which dinosaurs would be realized as both animatronic and CG characters, and which would require CG representations only, had already been worked out among Spielberg, Winston, and Muren by the time the dinosaur designs were being rendered. "We had been there before with *Jurassic Park*," Winston noted, "so we all had a pretty solid understanding of what could be done live and what would have

the creative departments, but especially so for Dennis Muren and the team at ILM, who could not start building computer models until the Winston dinosaur designs had been completed and approved. Yet, even at this early stage, Muren was evaluating shot designs, looking over the storyboards and engaging in discussions with Spielberg. "From Steven's point of view," Muren remarked, "the most important part of our involvement at the time was coming up with ideas for each of the shots. From my point of view, however, the first and foremost concern was, 'How are we going to make our work on this show better than it was on the first one?' The shot designs were

Photoshop rendering of gatherers watching the roundup sequence.

to be CG. It was very clear that there would have to be both live and CG raptors, for example, as well as both live and CG T-rexes, stegosaurs, and compys. We didn't know exactly how *much* CG would be required, since that depended, to some extent, on what we got from our creatures once we were shooting—but we knew there would be at least some CG work for every dinosaur." Full-motion dinosaurs that would be created through CG alone included the gallimimus and the mamenchisaurus.

Among the scenes that would rely heavily on computer animation was the roundup. Specific close-ups of the pachycephalosaurus interacting with hunters and their vehicles would be captured with Winston's mechanical creatures; but the dynamic nature of the stampede and the large number of animals in the scene could only be realized through computer graphics techniques. That action included shots of the smaller pachycephalosaurus and gallimimuses—as well as the hunter vehicles and motorcycles—moving in and out of the legs of the massive mamenchisaurs and parasaurolophuses. "During storyboarding," Dennis Muren recalled, "I had taken in a painting by John Gertche, an excellent dinosaur illustrator. In this painting there were different scales of ani-

mals interacting with each other. I have always loved the idea of contrasting scales, the big and the small in the same scene, and I suggested we do something like that in the roundup." At this point, full-body shots within the stegosaur sequence, the T-rex-versus-the-trailer sequence, the rex raid, the compy attack, the raptors in the grass scene, and the raptor chase in the abandoned town, were also on the CG agenda; and more shots would be added as the storyline developed and took some unforeseen directions.

As Muren and his crew at ILM prepared for their computer animation task, a different type of computer graphics assignment was being implemented within the Amblin art department. In November, Rick Carter returned from his first location scout, bringing with him photographs of the various sites that had interested him; and immediately after Thanksgiving, illustrator Stefan Dechant joined the *Lost World* team to manipulate those photographs within a computer as a means of creating location concepts. During his tenure on the show, Dechant would also digitally produce a series of two-dimensional, animated storyboards.

Although the digital tools had been far less sophisticated, Dechant had performed a similar service for *Jurassic Park*, using a Video Toaster effects system to create quick and crude video animatics. Now, armed with a more sophisticated yet still fairly simple computer system, Dechant again applied his artistic and computer skills to the creation of 2-D photo-storyboards, animating specific sequences to clarify the action in a way inked storyboards could not.

Dechant started with the rex raid, scanning in all of the completed storyboards for the five-minute-long sequence, then animating the two-dimensional images. "It was a fairly fast approach," Dechant explained, "because all of the images were in 2-D rather than 3-D. These photo-storyboards were not meant to be exact representations of final shots. They were just a different kind of visualization, an extension of the drawn storyboards that would give everyone a clearer sense of the action." Working on the photo-storyboards from November to March, Dechant ultimately animated not only the rex raid, but also the head-butting scene, the raptors in the grass, and the scene in which the stegosaurus attacks Sarah.

When not working on the 2-D animatics, Dechant was computer generating location illustrations by scanning in the photographs from Rick Carter's location scouts, then manipulating and enhancing them. "I combined Rick's photographs in Photoshop," Dechant explained, "then painted on top of them, adding dinosaurs or vehicles. That created a different kind of illustration, something to sell a particular look for a location rather than suggest action. These illustrations said: 'These are the surroundings. This is how big something would be in this environment, and here is our action taking place in that environment.' But they didn't define the shot or the action or camera angles. They were also a way to piece together an ideal location, taking elements that Rick liked from one place and adding them to another."

In addition to their conceptual purposes, the digital illustrations and storyboards served to stimulate ideas and reignite enthusiasm among all of the artists on the design team. Burnout was a real concern to Rick Carter, since, by the time the December 1995 holiday break had arrived, the art department crew had been working full-time on *The Lost World* for four months—and the show was not yet in official preproduction. "What Rick does best is inspire people," Dechant observed. "It was a tough show, and everyone was working really fast and really hard; and at some point it was easy to say, 'I've had it—I'm too tired to do this anymore.' But Rick was always able to rally the troops. He'd tell us, 'This is your chance to influence the movie. Steven will either like it or dislike it—but let's keep moving forward.'"

There had been little publicity that fall to alert the world to the fact that the sequel to *Jurassic Park* was in such a furious state of creativity. In fact, few outside the film industry would have known that a sequel was being planned. But then Crichton's novel was published, and not surprisingly, it rose to number one on the bestseller lists soon afterward. With the title now thrust into the public consciousness, Amblin and Universal considered the timing to be perfect; and on Thursday, November 9, 1995, the companies put an end to months of rumor and speculation by officially announcing that Steven Spielberg would be directing *The Lost World*, the big-event summer movie of 1997.

CHAPTER 3

DECEMBER 1995:
LOS ANGELES

Close to Eureka

With the onset of the holiday season, the feverish pace of design and development for *The Lost World* slowed, at least temporarily. For many, it would be the last respite until the end of principal photography a year later.

Rick Carter maintained his pace, however, leaving for another scouting trip to New Zealand in December, and narrowing his search to more specific areas of the country. To handle the logistics that would be entailed in the location shoot, location manager Peter Tobyansen was also brought onto the production in December. "Rick was still in New Zealand around Christmas," Tobyansen recalled, "and then, in January, we got together and started dealing with conceptual issues, discussing what the look of these environments was going to be. After that, it became a matter of, 'Where can that look be found?' And finally, 'Is it practical or even feasible to use this location or that? Can we get into these locations and do what we have to do? Can we put a large crew up in the area?' It's great to talk about exotic locations; but, at some point, you have to face the practical issues."

An exotic location that had been given a tentative thumbs-up was New Zealand.

"They really wanted the wild, volcanic look Rick had seen in New Zealand for the opening scene with the little girl on the beach, and—at that time—for the roundup scene," Tobyansen said. "But the idea was to limit the New Zealand shoot to those two scenes and a few establishing shots. It was too remote a location to shoot there for four months." Comparing location photographs of the New Zealand landscapes with images of Northern California, Tobyansen agreed with Carter's initial view that state parks in the vicinity of Eureka could work as a relatively nearby stand-in. "With the giant

The majesty of the Redwood forest.

Eureka! Humboldt County Film Commission

Above: After numerous location scouts by Rick Carter, parks near Eureka, California, were chosen for the film's exteriors. Producer Jerry Molen is flanked by state park officials Bob Anderson and Ken Anderson who were instrumental in securing sites for the production. *Right:* Artist David Lowery created this image for the crew T-shirt.

trees and the moisture and moss over everything, the place had a real primitive look to it—just like New Zealand had."

The Eureka-area photographs were intriguing enough to prompt a call to state park ranger Dan Scott, with whom Tobyansen arranged a scout in early February, which would include Rick Carter, Jerry Molen, and Colin Wilson. The purpose was not only to see what kinds of environments might be available, but also to determine if Eureka proper would be able to accommodate a crew of 150-plus people. "I had to put a whole package together before we could present this location as an option to Steven," Tobyansen explained. The quick trip to Eureka proved remarkably fruitful. "We hit an absolute bonanza there. We found a variety of locations that would do the job for us—and they were all within a forty-five-mile radius. Once Rick, Jerry,

Colin, and I had determined that we liked the look of the place and that we could house the crew there, we gave a presentation to Steven and Kathy Kennedy."

Eureka was now a serious location possibility; and within a few weeks, Carter and Tobyansen returned to the site, this time with Spielberg, Kennedy, and Dennis Muren. At the suggestion of a park ranger, Spielberg and his wife, Kate Capshaw, ventured out of the immediate area and drove the nearly fifty-mile jaunt to the Avenue of the Giants, a stretch of highway through some of the oldest and most magnificent of the redwoods. "Steven came back the next day," Tobyansen recalled, "and he was absolutely blown away by the beauty of those trees. He asked Kathy Kennedy, myself, Dennis Muren, and Rick Carter to go down and look at the area and see if there was any way we could put these giant trees in the film. It was about a forty-five-minute drive and the atmosphere in the car was very lighthearted. And suddenly, Kathy said, 'What are we all doing up here? Why are we all in Eureka, of all places?' And Dennis Muren said, 'Because when we said 'Costa Rica,' Peter Tobyansen thought we said 'Close to Eureka.' It was a funny moment, and that became our motto: 'Not Costa Rica…*Close to Eureka!*'"

Not only did Spielberg approve the location, he was so taken with its ambience and filming potential, he shifted some of the scenes that had been slated for the New Zealand shoot to the more accessible Northern California area. "We had thought we would have to spend three or four weeks in New Zealand in order to capture the kind of primordial look Steven wanted," Colin Wilson said. "But when we saw what the Eureka area had to offer, we decided to go to New

Zealand for just a few days to do the majestic vistas and the big opening shots. Essentially, it would be a second unit, but with a unique second unit director—namely, the same guy that was directing the first unit. For all of our main unit stuff, we would shoot in Eureka for about three weeks, right at the beginning of the schedule."

While Eureka and New Zealand were intended to provide most of the rich and forested Isla Sorna exteriors, much of the film would be shot within Southern California locations and on the Universal Studios stages and backlot, where all of the necessary sets would be constructed. With principal photography now just eight months away, a team of set designers joined Carter's production design effort, which launched into high gear right after the first of the year.

Supervising art director Jim Teegarden —who had often acted as Carter's right-hand man—kept tabs on the set designs as they evolved, while a handful of illustrators and set designers were assigned key design projects: Paul Sonski, assisted

by set designers Linda King and Pamela Klamer, was charged with the worker village; John Berger concentrated his design efforts on the gatherers' base camp; Sean Hargreaves worked on the hunters' camp; and Lauren Polizzi concentrated on the third act sets. Illustrator Matt Codd contributed to a variety of designs—including the T-rex cave, the InGen amphitheater, the dinosaur graveyard, and the worker village. Stefan Dechant was given the lead role in designing the T-rex nest, where members of the hunting expedition discover the baby tyrannosaur.

In addition, conceptual artist John

Above: A Matt Codd sketch depicting the expedition members trekking through the forest. The conifer-rich locale was an authentic representation of the real Jurassic-era environment. *Below:* A simple cut-out was often used as a stand-in for stegosaurus shots that would be computer generated later by Industrial Light & Magic. Spielberg on location with key members of the production team.

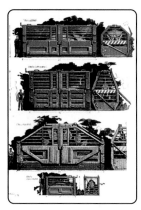

Top, left: Warren Manser at work on a design for one of the film's customized field vehicles. *Top, right, far right, above, and middle:* The well-funded hunter and gatherer expeditions come to the island equipped with state-of-the-art vehicles and communications systems.

Bell—who had designed the customized tour vehicles and other hardware for *Jurassic Park*—worked from his home base in Northern California to provide designs and blueprints for the hunter and gatherer expedition vehicles, while Pamela Klamer designed the modular, customized trailer used for the expedition's base camp.

Of the movie's few sets, the most sprawling was the abandoned town—the site of the raptor chase and helicopter rescue near film's end—which would be erected on the Universal Studios backlot. Throughout the storyboarding process, the town's design had continued to evolve in order to accommodate new ideas and sequences. "At one point," Matt Codd said, "there was going to be something like a Denny's in the middle of the town—the point being that the western world gets involved *everywhere*. We didn't want to stick to the idea of an old South American town; so we plopped in modern, western elements for contrast. It was also designed to make the point that the town had been abandoned for some time and that nature—including the dinosaurs—had reclaimed it. So there was

a lot of overgrowth in our illustrations."

One element of the town set that did not change throughout the design process was the large laboratory building sitting on a rise, overlooking the smaller buildings below. "The lab was meant to dominate the whole town, since it was the reason for its existence," Codd said. "At the opposite end of the town was the geothermal plant, which was supposedly how they powered the technology and the town." Between the lab at one end and the plant at the other were buildings such as a kiln, a boarding house, a gas station, and a maintenance shed. Immediately outside the town's main

Resting beyond the perimeters of the lab compound is a dinosaur boneyard. Two views of the boneyard, as depicted by Matt Codd.

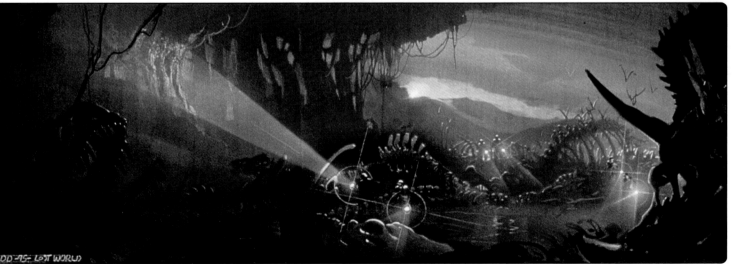

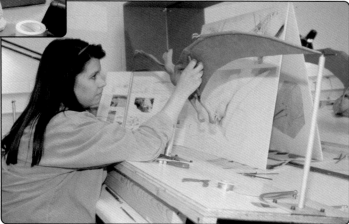

Opposite, clockwise from top left: Chris Robbins, Mark Maitre, Rob Ramsdell, Ian Stevenson, Jim Charmatz, Paul Mejias, Mark Maitre, Mark Maitre, Shane Mahan, Ursula Ward, Jackie Gonzales, Christian Lau, Tim Larsen. *Center:* Mark Jurinko.

Once maquettes were approved, artists and technicians at the Stan Winston Studio began building the mechanical creatures. Full-size sculptures were molded for the production of foam latex skins. *Clockwise from left:* Dave Grasso, Jackie Gonzales, Christian Lau, Ken Brilliant, Jon Neill, Joey Orosco, Bill Basso, Tim Larsen.

gates and adjacent to the geothermal plant would be the dinosaur graveyard, with massively-scaled skeletal remains thrusting upward. "The idea was to show a contrast between the dinosaur world and the man-made world. The camera would move past this bone yard, revealing a transition from bones to the pipes of the geothermal plant."

While the expanded design team devel-oped the movie's various environments and sets, other elements of the production were also starting to congeal. David Koepp's initial draft of the script was delivered to Spielberg on January 26—the first of nine drafts that would be submitted before the start of shooting in September. At the same time, Dennis Muren and the ILM crew were ramping up their involvement in the project.

Stan Winston Studio crew members at work on compy, the full-size T-rex, the parasaurolophus, the stegosaurus, and the pachycephalosaurus. *Clockwise from top left:* Jim Charmatz, Trevor Hensley, John Rosengrant, Ian Stevenson, Rob Ramsdell, Mark Maitre, Scott Stoddard. *Middle photo, clockwise from left:* Ken Brilliant, Ian Stevenson, Rob Ramsdell, Paul Mejias, Jackie Gonzales.

"That was the point at which we really started coming up with a plan," Ned Gorman recalled. "We nailed down what the new creatures were going to look like, what CG models could be reused from the first film, which ones would have to be built new, and what new painting schemes were going to be needed."

Also on the table was discussion regarding how interactivity between the CG characters and the environment might be orchestrated. "We wanted to see the CG dinosaurs splashing through streams and knocking branches off of trees, that sort of thing," Gorman explained. "So we went through the boards, specifically looking for places where we could incorporate interactive effects. We also talked specifically about the execution of the on-set gags, reckoning back to what had worked on the first movie and what hadn't. Things that had

Winston crew members make castings from the full-size sculptures in preparation for molding. *Bottom images, clockwise from left:* Dave Perteet, Grady Holder, Mike Harper, Beth Hathaway, Mike Harper, Grady Holder, Christian Lau.

worked the first time around would be improved; and things that hadn't were jettisoned so that we could come up with better, more elegant solutions."

January also brought with it an intensifying of the dinosaur build at the Stan Winston Studio. *The Lost World* not only presented the studio with new artistic challenges, it also threw down the gauntlet in terms of mechanical requirements. For the first time, the studio would move away from its heavy reliance on cable-actuated mechanisms in favor of state-of-the-art hydraulics.

The new approach had been initiated

The dinosaur characters were equipped with mechanical understructures by Kurt Herbel. Hydraulic mechanisms incorporated into a steel armature were engineered to drive the over ten-thousand-pound T-rex. Armatures built for the first film were refurbished to accommodate updated hydraulics that were smoother, more powerful, and more reliable.

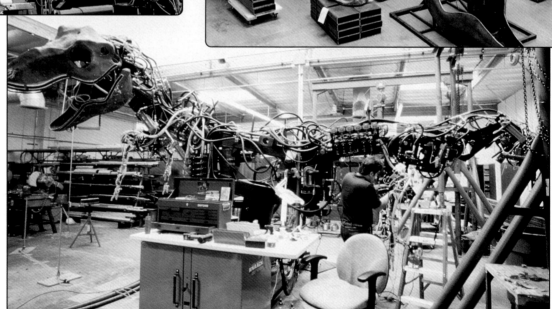

with the building of the T-rex for *Jurassic Park*—a fully hydraulic character that had necessitated a long and somewhat torturous learning curve, along with intense consultation with hydraulics engineers from the world of theme park attractions. Now, three years later, one of those consultants, Lloyd Ball, was a full-time Winston Studio employee and the in-house hydraulic engineer. Hydraulic designs were overseen by hydraulics department head Tim Nordella, and implemented by a studio mechanical department that had become increasingly proficient in the art and science of hydraulics. "People are very aware of the advancements in the computer world since *Jurassic Park*," Stan Winston commented, "but they tend to forget that the animatronic world has also made incredible advances, producing characters in which the technology is virtually undetectable. In large part, that is due to the tremendous advances we made in the first *Jurassic Park*, and in the time since then."

"In the three and a half years that passed after the first movie was made," Colin Wilson elaborated, "there were tremendous developments in hydraulic technology—developments that allowed us to manufacture twice the number of creatures in half the amount of time, and for slightly less money. That was quite amazing. We got a lot of improvements in performance and technology; we got double the number of characters; and we paid less for it. But the most important part of that equation was how much better the character performances would be for this movie."

Those improved performances would be facilitated by an innovative control system devised by the Winston engineers for *The Lost World*. Previously, articulation of the animatronic characters had been

Top: The baby stegosaurus under construction by Dave Grasso and Judy Bowerman. *Below, left:* An innovation implemented for *The Lost World* was a telemetry system that controlled a separate hydraulic unit, which in turn controlled cables connected to the character's internal mechanisms. Christopher Surft runs the raptor through its paces via the telemetry device. *Below, right:* Richard Landon adjusts the skeletal under-structure of the baby T-rex.

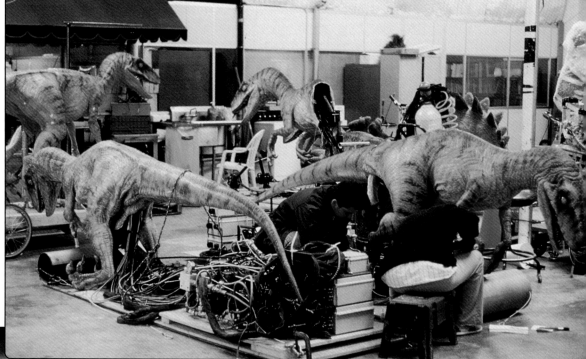

Right: Several versions of the mechanical raptors were designed and built, including full-body characters and insert heads. *Below:* Jeff Edwards at work on the armature for the pachycephalosaurus.

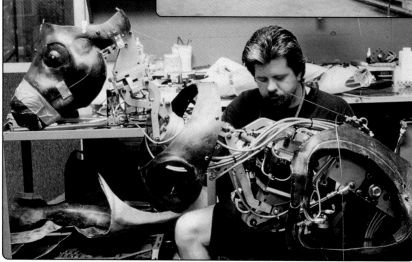

achieved by mounting mechanisms inside the bodies, operated by teams of puppeteers, either through cable or radio controls. Common problems included insufficient space within the smaller characters—limiting the size and number of mechanisms that could be employed—as well as slow reaction times due to the length of cable that ran between the operators' handheld controllers and the rig itself. Another major problem with the cable-controlled approach was that it required a large number of puppeteers, making it very difficult to coordinate a unified, harmonious performance.

Due to its massive size, the T-rex in *Jurassic Park* had been built and operated differently, with larger, stronger hydraulic mechanisms mounted into the creature's understructure. Those mechanisms had been electronically connected to a telemetry device—a small-scale replica of the T-rex armature that could be manipulated to actuate the movement and performance of the full-size rig. A movement on the head of the telemetry device, for example, would be immediately translated into an identical move on the head of the full-size T-rex.

The control system had worked like a dream. "We found, oddly enough, that our biggest and most difficult job on the first movie, the T-rex, ended up being one of the more practical and efficient characters, as far as performance went,"

Winston observed. "The telemetry device worked very well, and smoothly and efficiently—whereas the smaller characters, for which we'd relied on standard cable-actuation, required nine or ten puppeteers on controls trying to coordinate a move. It was very difficult to create a performance with ten people operating different parts of the head and body."

Encouraged by the reliable performance of the T-rex telemetry setup, Winston opted to use the same system for the dinosaurs in the sequel, but with an added twist. "For *The Lost World*," said Winston, "we decided to use a combination of the telemetry and cable-controlled techniques. It was an entirely new methodology—and something I'd been thinking about for a long time." The combining of techniques resulted in a unique system in which hydraulic mechanisms were assembled as a unit *outside* the body of the character, then linked to a telemetry armature at one end, and to the character at the other end, both through cables. A puppeteer's manipulation of the telemetry device would actuate the cable-linked hydraulic unit; which in turn would actuate the full-size puppet. "The big difference was that the cable-actuation was controlled by this external hydraulic unit, rather than by hand. And that hydraulic unit was hooked up to the same kind of computer-controlled telemetry device we had used on the T-rex for the first show. Each one of our characters had its own telemetry device that sent the signal to the hydraulic unit, which controlled the cable. The only reason we needed the cable at all was because the hydraulics were too big to fit inside some areas—although they did fit in the larger animals and in the larger areas of other animals. By putting the

hydraulic mechanisms on the outside of the bodies, we were no longer limited in the number or size of mechanisms we could use, and that translated to a much better performance. With this control system, all of the movements were more spontaneous, cleaner, and each character had a broader range of movement." Another advantage to the new system was that it cut down considerably on the number of puppeteers required for the operation of each character. "We still had to have several puppeteers to operate the telemetry device—maybe one on the head, one on the tail, and one just for facial expression—but we didn't have these large groups of performers trying to coordinate one single movement. That simplified and improved the puppeteering a great deal."

With the new mechanical control system devised and the painted maquettes approved for most of the characters, by February the studio was ready to shift into high gear in the building of the dinosaurs, a process that would begin with the sculpting of the new characters or, in the case of the returning dinosaurs, the refurbishing of existing armatures.

Although the T-rex had been sculpted and molded for the first movie—making the resculpting of the character unnecessary—some additional sculpture work was required to create a male version that would be distinguishable from the female. "Even though the male would have different coloring," explained effects supervisor Shane Mahan, "we were concerned that, under certain lighting conditions, the color would be canceled out, making it very hard to tell the two rexes apart. So, on the computer, I started manipulating photographs of the original T-rex. I did a series of eight different head shapes, all of which were submitted to Steven so he could make his choice."

Spielberg approved a male T-rex head that had an added neck wattle, a more prominent brow bone, and a battle-scarred face. "There is a lot of science now to support the idea that carnivores like the T-rexes would have been really scarred up," Mahan said, "with broken arms and legs and teeth knocked out. It makes sense, because they would have been battling each other for food all the time. In this film, the animals were in a more natural, wild environment, rather than the safe containment of the man-made park, and that would mean scarred bodies. Between the battle scars, the extended brow line, and the neck wattle, the male was a really distinctive animal." Rather than sculpt an entirely new head, Mahan and his crew took impressions from the original T-rex molds and sculpted the structural changes on top of them. "It was basically done like any character makeup we would do on an actor. We took a life-cast of the original, sculpted this new look on it, then molded up brow and neck wattle appliances that could be

Intricate paint jobs and layered resin eyes (below) resulted in stunningly realistic-looking characters.

added onto the completed rex head after the fact."

As Mahan restructured the cosmetic appearance of the male T-rex, Tim Nordella worked on modifying the mechanical steel-and-aluminum armatures that had been employed in *Jurassic Park*. Although only one T-rex character had made an appearance in the first film, two armatures had been built—one for a full-body rex and another for an insert-head version. With some modifications, the armatures would serve as the under-structures for the male and female T-rexes in *The Lost World*, both of which would be built only as forefront bodies. "Rather than build a full head-to-tail character," Winston noted, "we only had to build from the head to about mid-torso, including the small front appendages."

Unlike the full-body T-rex built for *Jurassic Park*—which had been mounted on a flight-simulator type of motion platform—the two refurbished rigs for *The Lost World* would be attached to carts and mounted on dolly track on stage, affording fluid forward and backward motion. Between the cart setup and the advanced hydraulic actuations, the new T-rexes would be able to perform a far greater range of movement than those built for the original show. "Tim Nordella not only designed the T-rex armatures," noted effects supervisor Alan Scott, "but also the dolly carts they would be mounted to. The carts were designed to work on a track that would be laid down on stage. It was a captured-rail system, much like a roller coaster cart and track. Both puppets weighed about eighteen thousand pounds; but, with this motor-driven cart system, they would be able to travel across the sound stage at between five and eight miles per hour."

Because the male would be doing more heavy-duty stunt work, its refurbished armature was made primarily of steel, while the less active female was built of lightweight aluminum. "We use aluminum whenever we can get away with it," said Scott, "because it makes the rig so much lighter and so much easier to work with. For the female, we used the insert head armature from the first picture, changing it a bit to make it more responsive." At its full extension on the cart, each T-rex reached a length of about thirty-seven feet and a height of twenty feet.

The foam latex skins covering the mechanical T-rex armatures were run from epoxy molds that had been saved from the first film. "We didn't have to remold the T-rex," noted effects supervisor John Rosengrant. "For the characters that did require new molds, we used the same aerospace epoxies that we had discovered for our work in *Jurassic Park*. The beauty of epoxy molds is that the warpage is nil. We've used epoxy for our molds ever since *Jurassic Park*, and it has become a real mainstay in the industry. But it was a big deal at the time—really groundbreaking." Since *Jurassic Park*, the makeup effects industry had also made tremendous strides in devising new materials for the skins themselves. Various forms of silicone, in particular, had proven astonishingly lifelike in fashioning everything from a fat belly for Tim Allen in *The Santa Clause* to the fleshy, translucent facial areas of the gorillas in *Congo*—the latter a Stan Winston Studio project. But despite the studio's success with silicones, Winston and his supervisors agreed that standard foam latex—the same material employed for the dinosaur skins for *Jurassic Park*—would better serve the char-

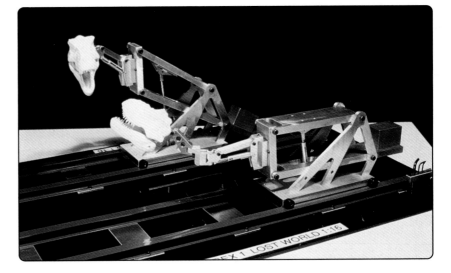

One-sixteenth scale model used to figure out the stage placement for the full-size version.

acters for the sequel. "Foam latex lends itself better to creatures as large as these, because it is much lighter than silicone, and it is easier to patch and repair."

One drawback to foam latex that had created tremendous problems in the first film was its capacity for absorbing water. Many of the T-rex scenes in *Jurassic Park* had been staged in torrential rainfall; and by the end of a work day, the foam skin had absorbed so much water, the extra weight threw off the delicate balance of the hydraulic mechanisms. To avoid the water absorption problems for *The Lost World*, the Winston artists sealed the foam rubber skin with a weatherproofing silicone coating. Finally, the skin for the male was painted in a new, vibrant color scheme devised by Rosengrant.

Like the T-rexes, the raptors did not have to be built entirely from scratch for the sequel—although new paint schemes for the males were devised by Chris Swift. Existing armatures were redesigned by Rich Haugen and Jeff Edwards to accommodate the new hydraulic control system, and stored molds were cleaned up for the running of new foam latex skins. At approximately six feet tall and thirteen feet long, the raptors would be operated both through hydraulics, for gross body movements, and cables for the more subtle actions of the head area. Four raptors were built altogether—two head-to-toe hero versions, and two head-to-mid-torso insert versions. In addition, the studio provided insert raptor legs—built by David Covarrubias and worn and operated by Rosengrant—that would be employed for low-angle shots of the animals' legs.

With the T-rexes and raptors slated for the middle to end of the production schedule, their refurbishing and modification could afford to proceed at a reasonably moderate pace. More pressing was the construction of the adult and baby stegosaurs, both of which were scheduled to be filmed in the Eureka area at the very beginning of production.

Mark Maitre and Scott Stoddard headed up a five-person team that sculpted and painted the adult stegosaurus, both in maquette form and full-size, while Al Sousa and Kirk Skodis took charge of its mechanical armature. The completed adult was nothing less than awe-inspiring. "It was absolutely huge," Rosengrant noted. "From the top of its spiny plates, it was about sixteen feet tall, and almost twenty-six feet in length. Just the girth of this animal was amazing. People would come into the shop and nearly drop when they saw it—'Whooaa!'" At eight feet long and about four feet tall, the baby stegosaur—sculpted and painted by Dave Grasso and mechanized by Bob Mano—was considerably smaller than the adult, yet still weighed in at three to four hundred pounds.

Another dinosaur slated for early filming was the compy, sculpted by Greg Figiel. A color scheme was rendered by Shane Mahan, and the final design was then turned over to the mechanical department. Although confident about his studio's ability to produce a character that was *aesthetically* pleasing, Winston harbored early concerns regarding the mechanization of the small creature. "It was so different than what was required for the large animals," Winston commented. "It was like going from building an eighteen-thousand-pound T-rex to building a watch. I was concerned about how much movement—especially quick, birdlike, attack movement—we would be able to get out of such tiny dinosaurs. The problem was how much we could get inside of it, in terms of mechanisms. Of course, we had already built a tiny puppet for the hatching baby raptor in *Jurassic Park*; but that puppet was slow-moving and very different in character than these dynamic compys."

Winston's concerns were put to rest when mechanical designer Chris Cowan devised a way to actuate the compys through a combination of cable-controlled servo mechanisms and pneumatics. "Chris came up with a new, brilliant approach to the compys," Winston said. "We'd used both pneumatics and cables before, obviously, but the process and methodology were new." Pneumatics controlled the tail, which could be made to whip around very quickly, as well as the eyes, which were mechanized by Jon Dawe, who had specialized in eye mechanisms ever since designing and building the orbs for *Jurassic Park*'s dinosaurs. "Mechanizing the eyes was an enormous challenge in itself. The compy heads were so small, there was very little room for an eye mechanism. Altogether, they were really amazing little characters, and we were able to get some incredibly wonderful movement out of them—well beyond my expectations."

Small, intricate mechanisms were required for the chicken-size compsognathus. Chris Cowan, who engineered the mechanics, and creature effects supervisor John Rosengrant prepare a test run-through for a scene in which the compsognathus attack hunter Dieter Stark (Peter Stormare).

Scott Stoddard sculpted and painted the eight-foot-long, five-foot-tall pachycephalosaurus, three versions of which would be built and employed: a full hydraulic puppet; an insert head; and one head-butter, built specifically to withstand high-impact action for the scene in which a pachycephalosaurus repeatedly rams a hunter vehicle. The hero pachycephalosaurus was among the most complex of all the puppets, and its mech-

anization fell to Jeff Edwards and Rich Haugen. "It had hydraulic moves, cable-to-hydraulic moves, pneumatic moves, and servo-driven moves," Alan Scott noted. "It was also built so it could be operated through wireless transmission for the scene in which the pachy is caught in one of the hunter snaggers during the roundup." The puppet's legs were pneumatically controlled to create some movement and life in the animal, even when it was stationary. "It also had pneumatic breathing, while all the facial muscles were servo-controlled. In fact, all of the dinosaurs had servo control for the faces. Servos are small and reliable, so they suit

For low-angled shots of the raptor, insert legs were built by David Covarrubias and operated by John Rosengrant.

facial control needs very well." Facial articulation would be operated by a puppeteer holding a joystick control.

The four-foot-tall, eight-foot-long baby T-rex was one of the most high-pressure builds on the Winston slate—especially when the construction timetable was moved up to accommodate the possibility, never realized, of shooting the character in Eureka. Not only would the baby T-rex have to be built fast, it was one of the most challenging creatures mechanically, requiring three different versions—including a totally self-contained unit—all built by Richard Landon and Matt Heimlich, from a sculpture by Joey Orosco and Bill Basso. The most complex of the three baby versions was the battery-powered, self-contained unit, designed to be operated through wireless transmissions. "Steven specifically asked for that because he wanted to see long-running shots of the characters carrying

this puppet," Alan Scott said. "We could have removed trailing cables digitally, but the actors would have been held up and limited by those cables during the actual filming." In some instances, a battery pack powering the puppet would be worn on the body of the actor carrying the baby T-rex. "We also built another self-contained baby rex puppet that was more lightweight and had only limited movement of the head and tail. It didn't have to be fully articulated because it was meant to be used in very long shots of Sarah and Malcolm carrying the baby." The third version was a hydraulic-and-cable-actuated puppet that would be employed for specific close-ups and insert shots.

In addition to the full-size articulated characters, the Stan Winston Studio was responsible for creating an eighteen-foot-long parasaurolophus carcass—sculpted by Paul Mejias in both maquette and full size—that would be seen in the T-rex nest sequence and in the dinosaur graveyard. For the scene in which the caged dinosaurs in the hunters' camp are freed by Malcolm, Sarah, and Nick, Winston team members Paul Romer, Tim Nordella and Lloyd Ball built a mechanical triceratops head. The same scene would feature a caged mechanical baby triceratops that had been built for the first movie by Shannon Shea and Alan Scott, but cut for narrative reasons before it was ever filmed. "We needed all these different dinosaurs in cages in the hunters' camp," Shane Mahan said, "and here was this baby triceratops, just sitting in storage. So we pulled it out and cleaned it up. It was actually in pretty good shape. We were able to use a lot of the original skin and original paint job." Alan Scott, who had originally mechanized the baby triceratops, oversaw the refurbishing of the mechanics himself.

By the end of February, the only dinosaur character whose construction had not yet been initiated was the pteranodon. Spielberg and Koepp were still struggling with the ending of the movie—in which the pteranodon was slated to make its appearance—and until those story issues were ironed out, Spielberg was reluctant to approve the animal's fabrication. It was a responsible position to take, considering the expense of building a creature with a six-foot head, a person-size torso section, and a wingspan of twenty feet. Ultimately, a pteranodon rendering by Crash McCreery would be translated into a full-size head and neck section, sculpted by Jason Matthews and mechanized by Kirk Skodis.

The construction of the dinosaurs for *The Lost World* was well under way as winter turned the corner toward spring. Stan Winston and his crew had already been hard at work on the project for six months when, at the end of February, *The Lost World* entered its official preproduction phase.

CHAPTER 4

Preproduction

With the onset of preproduction, Spielberg and his production team turned their sights toward casting. Preliminary casting efforts had been initiated in February; but now, with the shoot only six months away, it was time to make a more serious commitment to finding a cast for *The Lost World*.

Casting director Janet Hirshenson coordinated the task, working closely with associate producer Bonnie Curtis who, after working six years as Steven Spielberg's assistant, had recently been promoted. *The Lost World* would be her production apprenticeship. "I knew just enough about production to be dangerous," Curtis said. "But I discovered I had learned more than I realized in the six years I sat in the assistant's chair. And I couldn't have had better teachers for my first job as associate producer than Steven Spielberg, Kathy Kennedy, Colin Wilson, and Jerry Molen. They are all the best at what they do." One of Curtis' main duties, as she made the transition from assistant to associate producer, was casting. "Casting was something I had grabbed on to, even as Steven's assistant. It was something I always enjoyed, and I think I was good at it. Steven and I worked well together on that. He has a real talent for remembering faces, and I have a talent for remembering names. So, together, it worked."

Lists of actors' names for Spielberg's consideration had been arriving from Hirshenson since February; but with the script still in a state of flux, few casting decisions could be made. In fact, only one actor had been definitely signed at this early stage—Jeff Goldblum, who would reprise the role of Ian Malcolm. In *The Lost World*, Malcolm would be the story's central figure—a wiser man whose "excess of personality" had been subdued somewhat by his near-death experience in Jurassic Park and the difficult years that followed. So central was the character to the new film, and so indelibly connected to the role was Jeff Goldblum, the actor's commitment to the sequel had been secured before anything else progressed.

After *Jurassic Park*, Goldblum's career had continued on its soaring path with leading roles in the occult thriller *Hideaway* and the hugely popular *Independence Day*. When he was approached about starring in *The Lost World*, Goldblum did not hesitate to sign on. "Steven was spectacular to work with on *Jurassic Park*," Goldblum said, "and I had every good feeling about how that movie turned out. So when *The Lost World* came along, I was thrilled to have a chance to be a part of it. Many times when I'm considering a project, I'll list the pros and cons of doing it; and if I decide that, on balance, I can contribute

A Sean Hargreaves painting of the "Jurassic Park–San Diego" arena, a stateside attraction developed by the new InGen CEO as a means of salvaging the company.

The cast of *The Lost World*. *From left to right*: Jeff Goldblum as Ian Malcolm, Julianne Moore as Sarah Harding, Pete Postlethwaite as Roland Tembo, Arliss Howard as Peter Ludlow, Harvey Jason as Ajay Sidhu, and Thomas F. Duffy as Dr. Burke.
Far right: Goldblum with Lord Richard Attenborough, reprising his role as entrepreneur John Hammond.

something and that there are more pros than cons, I'll do it. But this was entirely positive. There were no cons. I couldn't have been more enthusiastic about it."

For Goldblum, part of the appeal of doing the sequel was that it would present the opportunity to bring something fresh to the role. "Malcolm has changed in the four years since he first toured Jurassic Park," Goldblum noted. "He's been through that first experience, and that's changed him. A lot of his mathematical orientation came out in the first movie. But in this one, he's thrust into this situation for very emotional, passionate reasons. Someone he loves is on the island, and he dives back into that dan-

gerous situation in order to save her. His reasons for being there in the first movie were colder, and more to do with scientific curiosity; whereas his reasons for being there this time are much more personal."

Goldblum's return as Ian Malcolm was a given. But since all of the other characters in the sequel were being introduced for the first time—with the exception of John Hammond, who would appear only briefly, and would be played again by Lord Richard Attenborough—the remaining casting decisions were wide open. One of the key roles was that of Sarah Harding, the expedition's paleontologist, and Malcolm's independent, sometime girlfriend. Three years previously—after

From left to right: Vanessa Lee Chester as Kelly Malcolm, Vince Vaughn as Nick Van Owen, Richard Schiff as Eddie Carr, Peter Stormare as Dieter Stark.

taking note of her brief performance in *The Fugitive*—Spielberg had arranged a meeting with Julianne Moore, an actress who had worked on stage, television, and more than a dozen films, including *Nine Months, Assassins,* and *Vanya on 42nd Street.* "The meeting wasn't for any specific role," Moore recalled. "Steven just wanted to meet me; so we sat in his office and talked. Then, a couple of years later, I got a phone call from my agent, saying Steven wanted to meet me again, this time in reference to *The Lost World.*"

Because Sarah would be such a physically demanding role, one of the topics approached by Spielberg in his initial discussions with Moore was her ability, and willingness, to meet those physical challenges. "He told me that he wanted Sarah to be very athletic," Moore said, "and he asked me about that—'You're pretty athletic, right? You can do that kind of stuff?' And I said, 'Yeah, I'm fairly athletic. I run every day, and I'm fit.' Of course, I had no idea at that time that I'd be rope-climbing and falling down hills and running through streams nearly every day." In his own mind, Spielberg had cast Moore even before this meeting; and, in fact, the director had encouraged Koepp to fashion the role of Sarah for her. The meeting only confirmed his decision, and Moore was offered the part immediately.

The two strong supporting characters who would complete the four-member gatherer expedition were field photographer Nick Van Owen—whose raffish exterior belies deep convictions regarding environmental issues—and field systems specialist Eddie Carr. Key players on the hunters' side were Roland Tembo—the big-game hunter after the ultimate prize—and colleagues Dieter Stark and Ajay Sidhu. Peter Ludlow, Hammond's bottom-line-driven nephew and InGen's new CEO, and Malcolm's thirteen-year-old daughter Kelly, would round out the core ensemble. Rather than go with star-power names, Spielberg and his casting team were determined to find excellent, solid actors who would fit into that ensemble and not detract from the overall film—a philosophy that had successfully guided the casting for *Jurassic Park.*

Between April and June the casting process intensified, and a number of actors were considered, met with, and eventually signed. Vince Vaughn, who had been seen on Warner Brothers Television's *77th Street* and in the low-budget film *Swingers,* was cast as Nick Van Owen, while veteran character actor

Richard Schiff signed on as Eddie Carr. Arliss Howard was pegged for the role of Peter Ludlow.

Perhaps the most multidimensional, complex character created by David Koepp for *The Lost World* was Roland. A gamesman and an intellectual, Roland had emerged from the script as a character whose fierceness is matched only by his personal integrity. The role called for an actor of tremendous presence—and Pete Postlethwaite fit the bill. Postlethwaite had been nominated for an Oscar for his supporting role in the movie *In the Name of the Father*, and subsequently played substantial roles in *The Usual Suspects* and *Dragonheart*.

As Roland's friend and tracker Ajay,

actor Harvey Jason would work closely with Postlethwaite throughout the shoot. A native of England who had come to New York with a play twenty years ago and had since made several stage, television, and film appearances, Jason had always wanted to work with Steven Spielberg. And so, when a call came from his agent asking him if he'd be willing to audition for *The Lost World*, Jason was quick to say yes. "My agent wasn't certain I'd want to audition," Jason recalled, "but I told him, 'For Steven Spielberg? Absolutely!'" Dieter Stark, Roland's cold, South African second-in-command, would be portrayed by Swedish actor Peter Stormare, who had made a strong and lasting impression on American audi-

Top, left: From a rescue helicopter, Ian, Nick, and Sarah witness the loading of the T-rex onto an InGen barge. *Top, right:* Roland and Sarah on Isla Sorna. *Bottom, left:* Dieter is confronted by a compsognathus. *Bottom, right:* Roland and Ajay prepare to enter the T-rex nest.

Both camps destroyed, the hunter and gatherer expeditions join forces to escape the island.

ences with his performance in *Fargo*.

Twelve-year-old Vanessa Lee Chester had been acting since the age of three in commercials and feature films such as *The Little Princess, Me and the Boys,* and *Harriet the Spy,* but a meeting with Steven Spielberg for a supporting role in the sequel to *Jurassic Park* was exciting, even for an old hand. "It was the biggest movie and part I'd ever come up for," Chester commented. "I met with Steven first and we just talked for a while. After that, I read with Jeff Goldblum, in front of Steven. And then I didn't hear from them for a long time, and I thought I probably didn't get the part. I was disappointed because I had wanted to be in an action movie *so bad*. So I was really excited when I found out, about three months later, that I got it. All I could think was, 'Whoa! *Dinosaurs!*'"

As Spielberg continued to meet with actors in his offices at Amblin, storyboards and set designs were being finalized in the art department annex across the street. Completed storyboards were mounted to a wall in sequence, so that the continuity of the movie—as it existed at the time—could be followed with a slow spin around the room. "It created a kind of visual script, a visual overview of the movie," Dave Lowery said. The story outlined in the storyboards that April would go through myriad revisions—some minor, and some so major that the final thirty minutes of the film would spin off in an entirely new direction. "It was a very big topic of conversation in the spring as to what was in and what was out, scenewise," Lowery explained. "We were trying to trim things because, as it stood, this was a four-hour-long movie. We realized, once we had it all together, that it needed some balance. It didn't all have to have this much scope and scale. So we started to look for where we could cut and where we really needed these big, spectacular beats."

In the course of trimming, the CG slate was pared down from 111 computer animated shots to a moderate 78—only twenty more than had been featured in the first movie. With a more concise picture of what CG shots would be required—and with the approval of Winston's dinosaur designs—the building of computer models was initiated at ILM by model supervisor Paul Giacoppo and modelers Dan Taylor, George Aleco-sima, Ken Bryan, and Doug E. Smith. "We were interested in improving the models considerably," Ned Gorman noted. "We wanted to make them less heavy and less data-intensive where we could, while recognizing where they needed to be *more* heavy and *more* data-intensive. Everything we did afterward—and most particularly, the animation—would depend on how these models were built and structured."

While new computer models were being built for the stegosaur, pachy-

cephalosaurus, compy, and parasaurolophus—all of which were based on maquettes received from the Stan Winston Studio—technical directors Patrick Neary and John Walker concentrated on updating computer models that had already been developed for the first movie, such as the T-rex, raptor, and gallimimus. Although no brachiosaurs would inhabit the new film, the brachiosaur model from the first film was also "retro-fitted" to serve as the roundup scene's mamenchisaurus. "This animal was unbelievably big," Colin Wilson noted, "so big, in fact, that scientists have not been able to figure out how it moved

Top, left: Sarah prepares to tranquilize the T-rex. *Top, right:* Sarah clings to a tiled rooftop during the climactic raptor chase. *Bottom, left:* Ian and Sarah confront Peter Ludlow. *Bottom, right:* Nick, Ian, and Eddie spot a stegosaurus herd shortly after their arrival on the island.

around. It was seventy to eighty feet in length, with a fifty-foot neck that jutted forward, arcing horizontally like a bridge—rather than upright, as in a brachiosaur. The shape of the head and body was similar, however; so ILM was able to modify the original brachiosaur model, stretch its neck out, and use it for the mamenchisaurus."

Artistic and technical issues were also being addressed over the animation of those models, an effort that would be guided by Dennis Muren and animation director Randy Dutra, a renowned sculptor, naturalist, painter, and stop-motion animator, *and* a key player in the CG animation for *Jurassic Park*. One of the challenges of that pioneering show had been finding personnel who could bridge the gap between the artistry of animation and the hardcore technology of the digital realm. *Jurassic Park*'s sophisticated computer animation had called for the services of animators who were computer savvy, *or* digital artists who possessed a talent for animation—but few had fit either profile.

As a stop-gap measure, *Jurassic Park* dinosaur effects supervisor Phil Tippett and his crew had developed a piece of hardware—dubbed the DID, for "dinosaur input device"—as a means of allowing traditional stop-motion animators to apply their skills to the virtual realm. Essentially a stop-motion armature—much like those used since the development of the animation technique early in the twentieth century—the DID was connected electronically to a computer. Each movement executed on the armature by the animator was translated directly to a computer model revealed on a monitor. Dutra had been the primary DID animator, and was responsible for much of the

animation for the T-rex-on-the-main-road sequence, as well as shots of the raptors in the industrial kitchen.

Now, the leap from stop-motion to computer animation had been made, and no such intermediary device would be necessary. What *was* still required, however, were the years of animation experience and animal behavior study represented in the person of Randy Dutra. During *The Lost World*'s preproduction, Dutra prepared for the upcoming animation assignment by scouring his own extensive library of documentary nature footage, culling animal walks, runs, and other behaviors to make up a ten-minute-long reference video. "There were specific behaviors I wanted to see in these dinosaur performances," Dutra explained, "so I assembled this video, pulling out the things I was looking for from hours and hours of footage. It was something I would be able to run for the animators, so they could get to the meat of the job right away. I also sent the video to Steven, so he could see what I was thinking and we would all be on the same wavelength." Through the video, Dutra broke down the behaviors of current species, relating them to the behaviors he wanted to see in the computer animation of the dinosaurs. "I pulled behavioral elements from elephants and rhinos for the stegosaurus, for example. For the compys, I wanted to see the kind of ritual, territorial head bobbings that some birds and even some mammals will do; and I had video of ostriches to demonstrate that behavior. None of these behaviors were a one-to-one kind of thing, though—'the stego should move like an elephant; the compy should move like an ostrich.' Dinosaurs weren't mammals as we know mammals today, and they weren't reptiles as we know reptiles today. They were unique. So, in all of these performances, we would be going for hybrids of different animals and different behaviors."

Several factors would make the computer animation assignment for *The Lost World* far more complex than it had been for its predecessor, one of which was the fact that a large percentage of the CG shots would feature not one or two animals, but large groups or even entire herds. "We started to apply all the knowledge we had acquired on projects such as *Jumanji* and *Dragonheart*," Ned Gorman explained, "sorting out what we had learned up to this point, in terms of modeling and animation, and figuring out

how all of that could be applied to scenes with multiple characters. That was going to be a big issue in this project. *Jurassic Park* had only six or seven multiple creature shots. In this show, nearly fifty percent of the shots would feature multiple characters."

Multiple creature shots, and Muren's commitment to improving the performances overall, were served by technological advances that would make all of

Top, left: Roland, Dieter, Ajay, and Ludlow at the sabotaged hunters' base camp. *Top, right:* Dieter and Carter (Tommy Rosales) prepare to round up stampeding herbivores. *Bottom, left:* Sarah, Ian, and Kelly are surrounded during the raptor chase. *Bottom, right:* Nick stumbles upon the laboratory compound.

"...*taste just like chicken!*..."

the computer processes more expedient. In addition, new software packages and techniques had been developed that would allow for more subtle facial animation and a heightened realism in the way an animal's skin moved over its bone structure and musculature. But as important as those advances were to the project, they did not add up to the kind of showy effects breakthrough that had amazed audiences upon first viewings of *Jurassic Park*. The technological leap represented by that film's computer-animated dinosaurs had been analogous to the leap from the horse-and-buggy to the first automobile. *The Lost World*, however, would be more closely related to the leap from an Edsel to a Mercedes Benz—

and no matter how ingenious or sophisticated the technology represented by the new model, audiences would not be likely to gasp, "Wow—there's no horse!"

"We'd come a long way with the technology since *Jurassic Park*," Dennis Muren mused. "And, even more importantly, we'd had a lot of time to learn how to do this, time to improve our understanding and artistry. Even with all of that, however, I knew we didn't have the same element of surprise and novelty working for us this time. And I knew that people might not have as big a reaction to the CG in this show as they'd had to *Jurassic Park*. But that's what we were going for, by making the shots just that much better."

CHAPTER 5

Countdown

The last five months leading up to principal photography signified a period of increasingly intense preparation. In April, department heads were hired and subsequently began to assemble their own crews. "Most of the people we hired were brought back either from *Jurassic Park* or other films Steven had done," Jerry Molen noted. "That gave Steven a comfort zone, I think, to know he had people who were not only very good at what they do, but whose first loyalty was to him and to his vision. It was truly a team and a family. By the first week in May, we pretty much had the entire crew committed."

Among those department heads returning to the *Jurassic Park,* fold including Jerry Moss in props and Christina Smith in makeup, was special effects supervisor Michael Lantieri. Lantieri had been a key player in many Amblin productions, including *Who Framed Roger Rabbit, Back to the Future II* and *III,* and *The Flintstones,* and had worked with Spielberg on *Indiana Jones and the Last Crusade* and *Jurassic Park.* For the latter film, Lantieri had provided special effects gags—such as the tour vehicle falling through the branches of the giant tree— as well as physical effects that created the illusion of on-set interaction with the computer animated characters. Ironically, some had seen emerging computer graph-

ics technologies as the future death knell for the field of mechanical and large-scale effects, since, hypothetically, CG would develop to a point that explosions, rainfall, flying cars, and tumbling buildings— all standard effects gags—could be more easily and even more convincingly created digitally in postproduction than they could live on a set.

But *Jurassic Park* had proven that not only would CG *not* supplant physical effects work, it would actually engender a whole new effects discipline geared toward effectively placing computer animated characters into their surroundings. For example, an early scene had a magnificent—and entirely computer generated—brachiosaur rising to feed off a leafy treetop. Lantieri's contribution was to make the real tree on location look as if it were being pulled and shaken by the feeding herbivore, a seemingly simple gag that had actually required impeccable timing. For another scene, in which a vehicle is crushed by a CG T-rex, it was up to Lantieri and his crew to rig the vehicle to collapse, as if being impacted. Lantieri had defined this emerging aspect of his work as "puppeteering the environment"—and with more and more movies featuring computer animated characters, his puppeteering skills became increasingly in demand. In fact, Lantieri had more work after *Jurassic Park* than he'd

An early version of the film's ending had a rescue helicopter being attacked by a pair of pteranodons. The ending was changed in favor of the San Diego sequence just weeks before the start of filming. Here, the pteranodon attack as depicted by Sean Hargreaves.

The expedition's state-of-the-art field equipment include a mobile lab trailer unit, specially-equipped hunter vehicles, and the gatherers' all-activity vehicles. A fleet of new sport utility vehicles were customized especially for the film by Mercedes-Benz.

ever had before the breakthrough film.

Lantieri had also been a vital link to the creature effects team for *Jurassic Park,* especially in regard to the massive hydraulic T-rex. The Winston Studio had been charged with designing, building, mechanizing, and puppeteering the character; but it had fallen to Lantieri to devise a means of mounting the ten-thousand-pound rig securely to the stage floor, as well as transporting it from one stage position to another.

As pivotal as Lantieri's contributions to *Jurassic Park* had been, however, they paled in comparison to what was asked of him for *The Lost World.* "Before we actually started and saw what this movie was going to be," Lantieri said, "I think many of us underestimated it. We'd done the first movie, so we all kind of thought, 'Been there, done that, no big deal.' But before too long, we clearly saw that we'd be doing five times the amount of work in this picture as we had for the first one. There was some advantage to having done *Jurassic Park,* of course—but everything in this movie was on a much larger scale. In the original, we had gags like the vehicle falling down through the tree, logs shaking and splitting for the T-rex-

on-the-main-road scene, and the big dinosaur bone display toppling at the end. Those were three pretty big sequences. But we would be doing that same amount of work in a single *week* for *The Lost World.* The sequences in this movie were not only bigger, they were tougher and much more complicated."

To meet the demands of the show, Lantieri expanded his permanent crew of twelve to include six additional members. The fully staffed effects shop began the *Lost World* project with the building of all the customized vehicles, including the gatherers' custom versions of the Mercedes Benz AAV—a vehicle design so new it had not yet been unveiled to the public when the movie went into production. Other vehicles that would be featured were customized motorcycles and military Humvees used by the hunters in the roundup. "Building the vehicles was a huge undertaking," Lantieri commented. "We had twenty different vehicles, each customized to serve specific functions for specific scenes or shots. Some were equipped with the snagger—the mechanical, multiarmed device the hunters use to catch the dinosaurs during the roundup—and we had to engineer that. Some of the

Costume supervisor
Sue Moore.

hunter cars had hydraulic-controlled seats that would swing out, or air bags that had to be rigged to inflate on cue. We spent months just getting the vehicles ready."

The two-module trailer for the gatherer's camp also had to be customized with a self-extending, rooftop communications satellite umbrella and high-tech equipment in the interior. The trailer would also be integral to one of the biggest effects sequences Lantieri's crew would face—the T-rex-versus-the-trailer scene in which the T-rex pushes the conveyance over a cliff. "The question we had to answer was: 'How do you drag 22,000 pounds' worth of trailer over a location or across a stage floor, make it jackknife, and then make it fall over a cliff and hang there by its boot?' We knew going in that sequence would probably be our most difficult of the entire movie."

Hired to act as liaison between all three of the effects units—Lantieri's crew, the Winston crew, and the ILM crew—was Michael Fallavollita. "I started by coordinating with Michael Lantieri and the art department," Fallavollita said, "making sure the vehicles were designed in a way

that would work for Michael's effects gags. Then, the job grew from there. Basically, they needed a person to be a pivot point for ILM and Stan and Michael."

Another returning crew head was costume supervisor Sue Moore, who would coordinate a six-person costume department. Moore began her assignment, as always, with extensive research. "To get me started in coming up with a look, I researched areas of Africa," Moore said, "specifically Mombasa, where a scene between Roland and Ajay would take place. I researched the people who work with animals in Africa, or do archeological work there. I also did research for the opening scene in the book, in which we see a yacht crew. Then I compiled all of this research in a booklet and sent that to Steven, to give him an idea of what my thoughts were for wardrobe. Another thing I did very early was break down the script into dramatic days so that we could gauge where we would need multiple costumes, and generally figure out the wardrobe needs."

John Villarino, a frequent collaborator with production designer Rick Carter, was hired as construction supervisor for *The Lost World*. Villarino had built the sets for *Jurassic Park* as well. But, whereas many of the sets for that film had been erected on tropical locations in Hawaii, most of the sets required for *The Lost World* would be constructed at Universal Studios, either on sound stages or on the backlot.

A key department head—and the person who would be working most closely with Spielberg during filming—was director of photography Janusz Kaminski. Unlike the majority of the crew, Kaminski was not a veteran of *Jurassic Park*. He had, however, worked with Spielberg before,

Art department wardrobe sketches.

Right and middle: The hunters' base camp was built on Stage 12 at Universal Studios. Here, the set under construction. *Below:* The completed hunters' base camp set as it appears in the film.

shooting *Schindler's List* in his native Poland. Kaminski's stark and gritty black-and-white photography for the film had earned him an Oscar for best cinematography; since then, he had served as director of photography for films such as *How to Make an American Quilt, Tall Tale,* and *Jerry Maguire.*

June marked the passing of a year since Spielberg had sat with Rick Carter and Dave Lowery at Dive! to first discuss visual concepts for *The Lost World.* After months of art department activity, those early ideas had now evolved into concrete set designs, location environments, and storyboarded scenes; and what had emerged was an overall look for *The Lost World* that was more raw, more primordial, than what had been imagined for its predecessor. "*Jurassic Park* had a very glossy veneer," Rick Carter noted, "but it became clear as the designs and the story evolved that *The Lost World* would be a rougher film. This movie was more about

Left: Both the T-rex nest and the "rex ravine" sets were built on Stage 28. *Below, left:* The rex ravine was erected around the white pillars in the background; the fixtures seen were from the original *Phantom of the Opera,* starring Lon Chaney. *Below, right:* Construction on Stage 12—which would be artfully redressed to represent various island locations—included the carving and painting of foam blocks to create rocky exteriors.

The lab compound under construction on the backlot at Universal Studios. In the background is the house used in Alfred Hitchcock's *Psycho*, a popular attraction on the Universal Studios Hollywood Tour.

just *surviving*. Unlike the first movie, there wasn't the luxury in this story to decide whether or not it was a wise thing to create these dinosaurs, or to wonder how everything got so out of hand—it wasn't about any of that anymore. It was just about not becoming lunch. So, whereas in the first movie the park was designed to look as if we had imposed order on nature with fences and roads and big gates, the designs for this movie evolved to reflect the fact that nature had reclaimed the territory."

The primitive, dark look of nature reclaiming its territory would be most evident in the abandoned village. Assistant art director Paul Sonski had started developing working drawings for the village in March. Those drawings were based on illustrations, storyboards, computer paintings, and a 3-D town model that had been in the works since the previous summer. As finally designed, the town was made up of thirteen buildings, including a laboratory, a geothermal plant, a schoolhouse, a gas station, a maintenance shed, and an enclosed kiln building designed specifically to accommodate one of the storyboarded action sequences. "We needed some kind of enclosed structure for the raptor chase," Sonski explained, "because Steven had developed this idea of Sarah being trapped inside, trying to dig her way out underground."

The path had been cleared for construction of the set with the completion of both the production schedule and the budget that June. "The budget was a little bit higher for this movie than it was for the first," Jerry Molen noted, "but only because of inflation. Just like gas prices or anything else, there were things that had increased in cost over the previous three years. But it was very close to our first budget—which was about $58 million—and we were actually able to get more for our money this time. We got more from Stan Winston and his people because a lot of the research and development had already been dealt with for *Jurassic Park*. We also got more from ILM, in part because the cost of CG had decreased. Also, Steven had decided to get as much as he could from the mechanical dinosaurs, without resorting to CG more than was necessary. So even though this movie would have a few more CG shots than *Jurassic Park*, it wouldn't have a great deal more.

"Steven was able to do that, to plan for it and budget for it, because he is such a visionary. He is able to see the entire movie in his mind long before he starts to shoot, so he knows exactly what he needs. He isn't the kind of director who ends up with a lot of film literally on the cutting room floor. There is no waste. Because of that, we were able to budget this movie very carefully and responsibly."

The schedule hammered out by Molen and Colin Wilson set the start of produc-

tion in the Eureka area on Tuesday, September 3, 1996. Filming would continue there into the third week of the month, then move to various stages at Universal Studios, where the production would remain throughout most of the month of October. At the end of the month, scenes in the worker village would be filmed. November and the beginning of December were scheduled for remaining stage work and nearby location shooting. Finally, the shoot was to conclude with a small unit going to New Zealand in the middle of December, with the film wrapping in time for the holidays.

By the schedule set down in June, only four and a half months remained until the company would be moving onto the abandoned town set; and so, construction of the town was under way by the end of the month. An empty, several-acre area on the Universal backlot had been chosen for the town site. "The idea was to keep everything contained on the lot so that it could be controlled," Colin Wilson explained. "Also, once we were finished shooting, Universal planned on keeping the set up and making it part of the tour. So, before we could really start building, they had to do a lot of grading in the area, laying in this concrete road to run the trams through."

At the end of June, stakes marking the various town buildings were laid out on the newly graded area, and wooden columns for the base of the lab building were erected. John Villarino's crews then broke for the Fourth of July weekend, assuming that the intended town construction would go into high gear when they returned.

It was not an accurate assumption.

At his vacation home in the Hamptons over the holiday, Steven Spielberg had

A Sean Hargreaves rendering of the scene in which the tranquilized T-rex is loaded onto the InGen barge for transport to San Diego.

suddenly seen an image in his mind—an image of a little boy looking out his bedroom window to find a tyrannosaurus rex drinking from the family swimming pool. The picture had not come totally out of left field; in fact, it was solidly connected to an idea for the third act of the film that he and David Koepp had been throwing around from the beginning of the project. Unwilling, up to now, to commit to the risky third-act plan, Spielberg—prompted by the little-boy image—swiftly made the decision to go with the idea, changing not only the course of the story, but of the production.

"We got a call from Steven that weekend," Paul Sonski recalled, "asking us how far we'd progressed with the town and how much construction had been done. He'd had an idea for the ending of the movie that would make the town less important, with a shorter raptor chase taking place among fewer buildings. Also, some of the money in the budget that had been earmarked for the town sequence was now going to go to this new ending. So the concept of the town was reduced to a laboratory compound, rather

than an entire village." Accordingly, the original thirteen buildings were pared down to include only the lab, the geothermal area, a small gas station, and the kiln.

Dave Lowery, among others in the art department, was not at all surprised that Spielberg had opted to change the original ending of the movie, which—following the raptor chase—had featured pteranodons attacking an airborne rescue helicopter. "No one was really convinced by that ending," Lowery commented. "Nobody bought it. It didn't have a grabber moment like the last movie did—the classic *King Kong* shot of the T-rex and the banner floating down. So we were pleased when we got the call informing us that Steven had come up with a new ending; and Rick and I immediately went out to the Hamptons to talk with him about it."

Spielberg's new idea had Ludlow and his InGen crew shipping dinosaurs stateside for the purpose of making them a major income-generating attraction. At the dock, the animal—or animals—would escape the hold and end up loose in a big city. To accommodate the new sequence, the originally boarded movie would be condensed from three acts to two, and the pteranodon attack would be eliminated altogether. "Everything up to the point where they leave the island was condensed into two acts," Lowery said. "Then, the new third act would involve dinosaurs—we didn't know how many or which ones—somewhere in America. It was a great idea to bring the action to a city in the United States, with the dinosaurs in our own backyard, as opposed to having everything happen on a remote island. Our only disappointment was that the pterodactyls got left behind. Rick, Colin, Jerry, and myself tried to convince Steven for a while to keep them in. We even called ourselves the Royal Pterodactyl Preservation Society, and we wrote an urgent plea to Steven on their behalf. Steven said, 'Thanks for the thought—but, sorry, no.'" Spielberg must have reconsidered at some point, since the final cut would include a brief appearance of a pteranodon at film's end.

Such a drastic narrative change was exciting and unsettling, both to the production design team and to David Koepp, who was now suddenly facing a major revision of the last third of his script—two months before the start of filming. "It was pretty hectic for a while," Koepp recalled, "especially since, when I first got the call from Steven, my wife was about five days away from having a baby. And then the baby came and I was trying to do this massive amount of work, writing a whole new ending. But even with all of that, I was delighted by the idea. In fact, from the very beginning, Steven and I had thrown around the idea of the dinosaurs making landfall, so to speak. We'd gone back and forth, recognizing that there

were good reasons to do it and good reasons not to do it. The main reason *not* to do it had been that if it wasn't done just right, we'd suddenly be remaking *Godzilla*. But over that Fourth of July weekend, Steven had come up with a way to do it right; and he called me to say, 'I think we've got to go for it.' It was a real wish fulfillment thing. With this kind of movie, you have to sit down and say, 'What would I want to see if I was in the theater? What are the sequences I would demand to see in this movie?' And a dinosaur coming into the streets of a big city was right at the top of that list."

Another selling point of the new ending was that it took the film in an entirely new direction—one that had not been explored in *Jurassic Park*. "We never wanted to remake the first movie," Koepp said. "We wanted to continue the story, and we felt that this idea was a logical extension. The original ending resolved the story just fine—but we didn't want 'fine,' we wanted 'outstanding.' My hope was that audiences would see the raptor chase in the town and the helicopter rescue, and they'd think the movie was over—'Well, that was pretty good. A little like the first movie, but good.' And then, here comes the knockout punch."

With Koepp's help, Spielberg's broadbrush scenario for the ending was soon filled in with much-needed detail: "A dinosaur" became the male T-rex, and "an urban environment" became the city of San Diego. "San Diego would be the logical port the ship would come into if it was coming from a Costa Rican island," Lowery commented, "and it is a city that's already associated in everybody's minds with animal attractions, because it's famous for its zoo and the Wild Animal Park. San Diego also has a very nice urban look to it, yet it doesn't look anything at all like New York or the other city skylines we've seen over and over again."

Having set up the premise of the T-rex in the big city, Spielberg, Koepp, and the art department began to toy with a barrage of ideas and images—some workable and some not. "We tried to imagine all the things the rex could do now that he was in an urban environment, as opposed to a jungle," Lowery recalled. "The Navy SEAL base is right there on Coronado Island, so there was some talk of doing a 'SEAL versus the dinosaurs' kind of thing. Eventually, ideas had to be winnowed down to something that was dramatic but manageable, and not too silly."

Koepp delivered the first draft of the new third act one week after Spielberg's call, but many revisions would follow before the scenes were filmed in November. As finally scripted, the new ending begins with the helicopter rescue of Sarah, Malcolm, Nick, and Kelly, who witness the heavily sedated male T-rex being loaded onto an ocean barge as they fly over the island. Ludlow's plan is to transport the beast to an InGen

"... it could use another P.A...."

amphitheater where it will be exhibited, becoming the company's new cash cow. Something goes wrong in transit, however, and the crewless ship crashes into the InGen dock in San Diego. The T-rex emerges from the hold and goes in search of its baby—which has been transported by helicopter to the InGen arena—invading the urban streets, ramming a city bus, and creating general panic. Finally, Sarah and Malcolm kidnap the baby T-rex and take it to the dock area in order to lure the marauding rex back onto a ship bound for Isla Sorna.

While Koepp was devising the new ending, all of the other departments were scurrying to accommodate the change in narrative. Paul Sonski and the set designers quickly redesigned the town to reflect its new designation as a lab compound. "When we redesigned it, we moved the lab building closer to the other buildings," Sonski noted, "while also changing some of the buildings and deleting others so that the layout was more appropriate to the condensed action. All the original drawings we had done were shelved, and we came up with new designs for every building, except the lab." The intent and design of the town had changed but, unfortunately, the schedule had not. In order to meet that schedule, the set still had to go under construction immediately, even as blueprints were being reworked and modified. "We were drawing and building at the same time in order to get this set up to speed. Since they already had most of the working drawings for the lab, they started construction at that end of town, and worked their way to the other buildings as we were designing them. John Villarino and his construction foremen worked very hard to quickly accommodate the new

plans." In the end, only the dinosaur graveyard and about one quarter of the originally designed town would be built for the show.

With much of the budget and shooting schedule now going to the San Diego sequence, the raptor chase also had to be pared down and, throughout much of July, new choreography for the chase was under discussion. "Steven didn't want to do too much at this point in the movie," Lowery commented, "because he wanted to save the big thrills for San Diego—not only in terms of emotional impact, but also in terms of CG shots. We couldn't blow our entire CG budget before we'd even gotten to the third act of the movie."

The hustle going on within the design and construction departments was mirrored in the effort by Rick Carter and Peter Tobyansen to find suitable locations for the T-rex's unguided tour of San Diego. A downtown San Diego high rise was eventually found for both exterior and interior views of the InGen corporate building; but for scenes scripted to take place on the streets of San Diego, the scouts began to look closer to home. "There was no point in shooting an alleyway in San Diego, one hundred miles away, when an alleyway in Manhattan Beach right next door would serve just as well," Tobyansen noted.

The new third act sequence required some deft regrouping at ILM as well. "The change in the ending was a big deal for us," Dennis Muren said, "but it was one I was all in favor of. I really liked the idea of bringing the T-rex to the city—even though we had all looked forward to doing the pteranodon scene, and we had already done some research into animating the flying shots. The biggest impact on us was that the raptor chase sequence was going to be shorter, and we were going to gain a lot of T-rex shots. It wasn't an even trade though, because we gained more shots than what we lost. At this point, our shot count began to grow a bit."

The team least affected by the new ending was Stan Winston's, since most of the T-rex-in-the-city shots would be computer generated. While other departments dealt with the revisions wrought by the change, the Winston crew continued to bear down on the dinosaur construction assignment. With the Eureka shoot now just weeks away, the pressure was mounting—not only for the construction of the rigs that would be shot there, but for every character on the dinosaur slate. From years of experience, Winston knew that once production started, there would be little time available for ironing out mechanical problems. "By the end of July," Winston recalled, "the adult and baby stegosaurs, the compys, and the pachycephalosaurus were done, and everything else was in pretty good shape. We were still working feverishly, though, and the crew was putting in very long hours."

As characters were completed, they were put through a series of tests and trial runs at the studio. Early in July the Winston crew had conducted a test of the hydraulic T-rex with stunt coordinator Gary Hymes, specifically to work out scenes in which the rig would have to interact closely with actors or stunt people. At the beginning of the test, the puppeteering crew relied on the memory playback feature of the hydraulic system, which had enabled them to set a complex move, record it in the computer's memory, and then play it back reliably time after time. The thinking was that the computerized memory function would eliminate human error in the puppeteering, thus making the interaction with the performers as safe as possible. "We thought we should reduce the variables as much as possible," Alan Scott explained, "because we were going to have this eighteen-thousand-pound puppet coming into contact with real people. By using the memory feature, we would know every movement the puppet was going to make because they would be repeated exactly every time. But in our test, we found that it worked so much better to let the stunt man lead the action—let him move and react, and then have the puppeteers, working live, make the T-rex move and react accordingly. It made for more believable interaction."

As preproduction counted down to the last four weeks before the start of filming in Eureka, preparations intensified throughout all of the departments. Immediately prior to the shoot, Jerry Molen and Colin Wilson conducted a technical scout of the chosen location areas. "We took the cameraman, his gaffer, and his key grip and walked the various locations," Molen explained. "It was a way to determine what equipment would be needed, so that once we were actually on location, we would have everything necessary to get the job done. In a small town like Eureka, there is no place to go if you suddenly find you're missing something important. We tried to eliminate that problem with the technical scout."

Rick Carter, Dave Lowery, and John Berger also scouted the area one more time in August. "Dave and I were going to be doing a lot of the art department work up there," Berger recalled, "so we took notes with Rick. It was a matter of us

The potentially dangerous T-rex rigs were put through numerous tests with the stunt crew to ensure actor safety during production, and to choreograph specific stunt sequences.

being on the same track—especially since Rick, at some point, would have to leave to get everything up to speed for the third act in Los Angeles. We had to come up with a coherent plan of attack." Danny Ondrejko and his greens crew also arrived early to check out locations and find nurseries to supply their needs. "In order to film in these parks, they had to work out what plant life they could bring in, what would be ecologically feasible. We

didn't want to bring in a lot of foreign organisms to disrupt the system there." Berger returned to Eureka for good on August 22, with Carter, Lowery, and art department coordinator Mark Kurtz arriving a few days later.

On September 3, 1996, the plane carrying the cast and crew of *The Lost World* touched down at Arcata Airport; and the following day, principal photography for *The Lost World* was finally launched.

CHAPTER 6

**SEPTEMBER 1996:
EUREKA**

Valley of the Giants

The first week in September, the cast and crew of *The Lost World* flew to Eureka via chartered plane and settled into their hotel accommodations. The crew numbered 150 and its members and mission were, inevitably, the subject of intense curiosity in the quiet town of 30,000 people.

Actual filming sites were situated twenty-five to fifty miles to the north, within specific areas of Prairie Creek Redwoods State Park and Patrick's Point State Park, both part of a coastal region that is home to old growth redwood forest, only 85,000 acres of which still exist on the planet. Coastal redwoods are earth's tallest living organisms, some reaching over 360 feet in height. Individual trees can live two to three thousand years, but the forest itself is 125 million years old—thirty times older than the Grand Canyon. Fittingly, the forest was born just at the end of the Jurassic Period, and at the onset of the Cretaceous.

Eureka and surrounding Humboldt County were not new to the business of filmmaking. In fact, the first production filmed there was 1918's *Valley of the Giants*, a movie remade in the same location in 1927, and again in 1938. The beauty of the forest coastal area had been tapped by filmmakers in the six decades since, for movies such as *Return of the Jedi, Jennifer 8,* and *Outbreak*. Now, dinosaurs were returning to the redwood forests.

The path had been cleared for the production through ongoing communications between location manager Peter Tobyansen, producers Colin Wilson and Jerry Molen, and Humboldt County film commissioner Kathleen Gordon-Burke, who was instrumental in securing the cooperation of officials from both the state park system and the adjacent Redwoods National Park, administered by the federal park system. "There were a lot of scientists that had to be consulted before the park systems would pass on filming here," Gordon-Burke said, "including entomologists, the fish and wildlife and stream scientists—all of them had to sign off on it."

Not too many years ago, such clearances would have been next to impossible to obtain. "The state parks people tended to be a little film-unfriendly in the past," Gordon-Burke said. "They were afraid that filming might adversely impact the area. The other problem was that each park made its decisions and its rules independently. There was no one standard

The gatherers flee from an angry herd of stegosaurus. This key sequence was shot on location in Humboldt County's Prairie Creek State Park.

Spielberg waits between setups on location in Eureka.

throughout the state. So the stringency of the rules in a particular park completely depended on the attitudes of the people running that park."

For many productions, filming in the state parks just wasn't worth the trouble, despite the beauty and richness they offered. But then, two years ago, when the economically crunched state of California began to realize that its once booming film industry was going elsewhere with more and more frequency, it quickly commissioned a book by California State parks assistant to the director Ted Hilliard, entitled "Filming in the State Parks," which standardized the rules and regulations for all of the parks within the system, and eased the clearance process considerably.

Much of the goodwill that would exist between the state parks and the *Lost World* company could be attributed to

Ken Anderson and Bob Anderson, two nonrelated Park Service officials assigned to oversee the production. On a day-to-day basis, film activities at the state parks were monitored by park rangers. "Working with Amblin took a lot less effort on our part than other companies," Ted Hilliard said, "because there was a strong sense of responsibility in this company. So even though it was a big crew— 150 people—we could accommodate them much better than we could a smaller, but less responsible crew. The Amblin people were extraordinary in their disciplined use of the area." The give and take between the production and the parks was exemplified by Jeff Goldblum and Julianne Moore agreeing to do public service announcements for the park system.

The three-week Eureka schedule called for both day and night shooting, which would be conducted at a variety of park locations. Day scenes included the compy attack on Dieter, the roundup, and Sarah's encounter with the stegosaur herd, while portions of the T-rex-versus-the-trailer sequence and various "trekking through the jungle" shots would be filmed at night. Each morning or afternoon— depending on the schedule—vans pulled up in front of two Eureka hotels to transport the crew to the locations, up to fifty miles north on Highway 101. Camaraderie built during the scenic twice-daily trek as crew members laughed and talked, commenting on the massive, ancient trees, the freshwater lagoons situated just yards from the Pacific Ocean shoreline, the quaint Victorian-style homes, or deer spotted at the side of the road.

Arriving at the ranger-manned kiosk at the park entrance, drivers were guided to that day's shooting area by a simple paper sign that featured only a rendering of a dinosaur and an arrow pointing the way. Curious park campers and local citizenry were hardly fooled by the "code"—but anyone hoping to follow the arrow and catch a glimpse of the crew in action was stopped by a friendly but firm law officer stationed at the closed roadway. On the day schedule, shooting typically began at six A.M. and wrapped at seven or eight P.M., with crew members returning to their respective hotels by ten. The schedule—or its night shoot equivalent—was the same, six days a week, for the entire three weeks.

The experience was a new and enlightening one for Dave Lowery, who, as a newly promoted assistant art director, was in on the day-to-day activities of a location shoot for the first time in his career. "Usually, a storyboard artist is done with a show by the time they start shooting," Lowery explained. "So this was very different for me." One of the most enjoyable aspects of the shoot for Lowery was being able to watch Steven Spielberg in action. "Steven once said that there are three stages of making a movie: the first is shaping the script; the second is storyboarding; and the third is the actual filming of it. Being there to watch him in the process of that third stage was very exciting. Steven seems to use the storyboarding phase as a way to solidify the action beats and the rhythms of scenes. But then, when he comes to shoot, he condenses those storyboards so that one shot makes three points. Steven is, above everything else, a shooter. He knows what he wants, and there is never any doubt with him. On some days, almost everything he shot was different than what we had storyboarded. He pushed things, added things, condensed things. It was

very exciting for me to be there and watch all of that happen."

"Steven has said that when he follows storyboards, he feels as if he's working at Denny's—just picking up orders and filling them, then going on to the next one," Rick Carter added. "Colin Wilson pointed out that it's a pretty high-class Denny's job—but Steven's point, I think, is that the more connected he is to what is happening with the camera right there at the moment, the better. For all that he does to prepare and plan, in some ways he doesn't really want to have all of his ideas cemented beforehand. Because, then, shooting is just going through the motions of fulfilling what he's already thought of, as opposed to discovering in the moment."

The art department's task in Eureka was to create the environments in which those moments of discovery could happen. Since there was little in the way of set construction—only ramps and platforms to accommodate frequently traveled pathways or particular camera positions—Carter, Lowery, and Berger spent the majority of their time ensuring that everything the camera was going to capture for any given shot looked aesthetically pleasing. Most of the actual set dressing, however, fell to the greens crew. "For each shot," Lowery explained, "the greens people were the last guys out of frame before the actors stepped in. Up to that point, they would be in there trying to make everything look fresh and undisturbed."

Considering the lushness of the redwood forest, the greens assignment in Eureka was surprisingly extensive. Additional dressing was required not only to create a richer, thicker ground cover, but also to provide camouflage for film

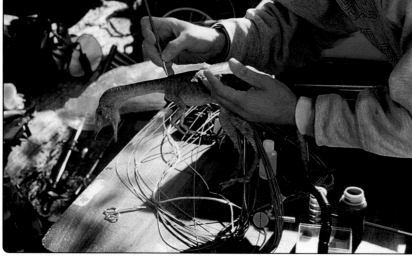

Top, left: On location in Fern Canyon, Stan Winston confers with Peter Stormare prior to filming the compsognathus attack scene. *Top, right:* Stormare in makeup, attended to by makeup supervisor Christina Smith and artist Matthew Mungle. *Bottom:* A Winston crew member readies one of a dozen mechanical compsognathus for the attack scene.

equipment, trucks, and generators. Palms and other nonindigenous trees were also judiciously incorporated to make the area look a little less like a redwood forest. "I've never been involved in a show that had such a huge greens assignment," Berger noted, "and the crew up there—Danny Ondrejko, Frank McEldowney, and Kevin Mangan—was incredibly good. Throughout the parks, there were pockets of alders and clearings and other pockets of redwoods and pines, so we were able to get a lot of different looks, right in the

same area. The greens we brought in helped to tie all of that together, so one location would blend with another." The greens crew artfully positioned both synthetic logs—built at the studio and transported to Northern California—and real foliage throughout location areas. "They also brought in bags and bags of natural forest ground cover," Lowery said, "to cover up areas where people walked and left shoe tracks. Since it was from the area originally, it was environmentally safe to use it there and spread it around."

The art department was responsible for preparing not only designated location sites, but alternates that could be used in case of bad weather—an ongoing concern in an area that receives fifty to eighty inches of rainfall annually. "We were working at the whim of the weather," Berger noted, "and at the whim of where the sun was or how overcast it was. We tried to prepare and provide options so that if we lost the sun at one place, we had another area all set up and ready to go for a different shot. Often, when we'd

Separated from the other members of the expedition, Dieter is attacked by a herd of compsognathus. *Left:* Peter Stormare is covered with Stan Winston puppets. *Below, left:* ILM digital story-board of the scene. *Below:* Early storyboard sketches.

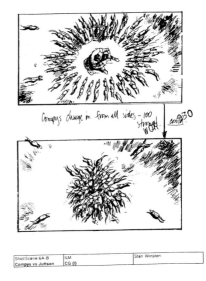

suddenly get a break in the clouds and the sun would come out, we'd change our plans and do other shots right then because we didn't know when the sun might appear again."

The first few days of the shoot were spent in Prairie Creek's Fern Canyon, a two-mile-long, narrow canyon enclosed by eighty-foot rock walls covered in ferns. "The rock weeped water, and there was a stream down the middle of it," Lowery said. "At its widest it was twenty feet, but it narrowed to about ten feet in some

places. It was crisscrossed with all of these logs—trees from above that had fallen down into the canyon. It was an extraordinary place." At Fern Canyon the principal photography crew captured the scene in which Dieter becomes separated from the combined hunter/gatherer group and, lost in the dense forest, is attacked and killed by a pack of compys. To shoot the scene, the Stan Winston Studio's dozen mechanized compys were attached to actor Peter Stormare, then puppeteered from off camera.

Full-motion versions of the compys would be inserted into the scene through computer animation. Dennis Muren, Ned Gorman, Randy Dutra, CG supervisor Kevin Rafferty, coordinator Vicki Engel, and match-move technician Jack Haye were all on hand that first week—as they would be throughout the shoot—for the filming of background plates into which the CG characters would be composited.

"One of the most important roles of a visual effects supervisor is what he does on the set," Muren commented. "That is where the shots can either fail or be raised to a higher level than what has been boarded. Once on the set, I was always encouraging Steven to come up with ideas that would make the shots more than they might have been, and to take bigger risks. A lot of directors are terrified to do something like that, but Steven is great about making those kinds of changes on the set."

The second week of filming was spent at Patrick's Point State Park, a coastal wilderness with bluffs overlooking the ocean and open fields that, a century ago, were used as farmland. The coastline at Patrick's Point would be filmed for specific medium shots of the Isla Sorna coast, then matched with wider establishing views shot elsewhere. The park also served as the location for the gatherers'

Above: In specially-equipped vehicles, the hunters round up a variety of herbivores for transport to Jurassic Park-San Diego. Features such as sidecars and snagger devices on the vehicles were engineered by special effects supervisor Michael Lantieri and his crew. Special camera rigs were mounted on during the filming. *Right:* Patrick's Point provided a spectacular setting for the gatherers' base camp. The characters watch as InGen helicopters invade the island.

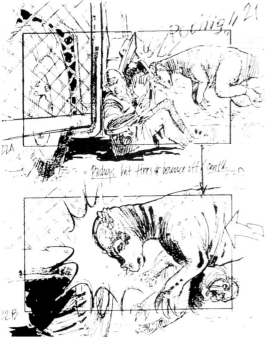

the parking lot was dressed to look like ground cover. It was a great spot because we were up high, looking out over the ocean, with rocks and trees all around. We shot scenes looking over the trailers, out toward the ocean; then, for the reverses, the camp would be set up on stage at Universal."

Transported to the site were the customized trailers that had been built at Universal, where existing chassis were modified with custom features by Michael Lantieri's crew. "It was actually one long unit," Berger explained, "two trailers connected by a flexible connector boot in the middle. The front portion was the mobile home, then there was the accordionlike boot section, and then the laboratory section at the back of the trailer." Once set up at Patrick's Point, the trailers were surrounded with appropriate set dressing such as additional foliage and synthetic foam logs.

In addition to the setting-up camp day scenes, some night exteriors for the T-rex-

trailer camp. "You see the trailer come in at Patrick's Point when they first set up camp," Peter Tobyansen explained. "We were actually in a parking lot—the place where visitors park so they can get out of their cars and look out over the point—so

Right: The gatherer expedition monitors the roundup from a high ridge. The scene was filmed on Ceremonial Rock at Patrick's Point. *Below:* The camera crew prepares to shoot a scene with Vanessa Lee Chester, Julianne Moore, and Richard Schiff.

versus-the-trailer sequence were shot at Patrick's Point, as was a scene in which the gatherers witness the hunter roundup from atop a tall ridge. "The actors were up on Ceremonial Rock," said Tobyansen, "which is a pretty famous spot at the park. It looks out over a big, grassy meadow. We took out all the guardrails on top of the rock to make it accessible for the camera crew, and shot the actors looking out onto the field—supposedly watching the roundup below. To get reverse angles of the actors on the rock, the cameras were positioned on a lower rock at the same location."

There had been talk of shooting the live-action plates for the roundup in the grassy meadow located at the site, but the production company was concerned about damaging park property. "We had a lot of heavy film equipment that would be in there," Tobyansen said, "as well as the hunter vehicles tearing around, so we gave up on the idea of actually shooting the roundup there." As an alternative, the company found a larger, privately owned field nearby. "Once we got to shooting the roundup, we were very glad we'd gone with this larger field. Steven wound up shooting it in a very broad, sweeping way—so there was no way the action could have been contained in that small park meadow. This field provided ample room for the kind of wide-ranging action Steven wanted for the roundup."

The week of roundup filming was a big

one for all of the departments, but particularly for Michael Lantieri's effects crew. Lantieri's shop had built and engineered the customized vehicles and motorcycles seen in the roundup, and it was the effects crew's responsibility to operate and maintain the vehicles during filming.

Stan Winston and his team were also front-stage that week, operating their mechanical pachycephalosaurus for the scene in which the seemingly benign animal destroys one of the hunter vehicles. Lantieri's crew was also intimately involved with the rigging of the mechan-

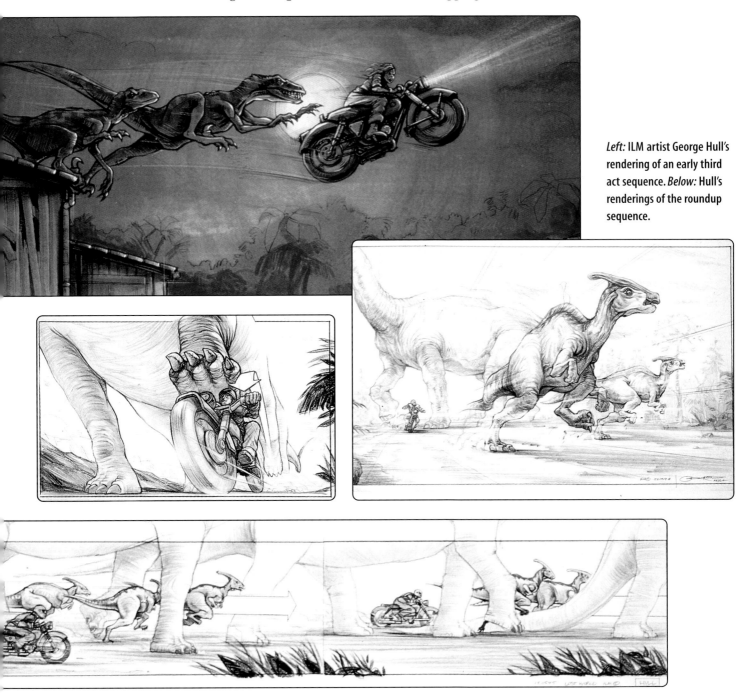

Left: ILM artist George Hull's rendering of an early third act sequence. *Below:* Hull's renderings of the roundup sequence.

ical pachycephalosaurus shots, particularly those in which the animal is seen struggling within the arms of the snagger.

Except for a handful of live-action pachycephalosaurus shots, however, the roundup stampede would be made up almost entirely of computer generated animals. "The most difficult part of shooting the roundup from our point of view," Dennis Muren said, "was that it had to have such a sense of vastness. There was going to be a stampede of running animals that was five hundred feet long, with vehicles going twenty to twenty-five miles an hour—so it was a real challenge

to figure out the timing of that. We had to solve those problems right there on the set, at the spur of the moment, because the dynamics were so complicated. It wasn't something that could be preplanned. We had storyboards, of course, but there was no way to know what was really going to

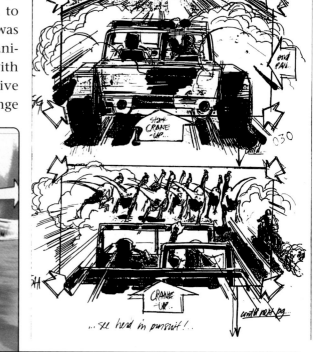

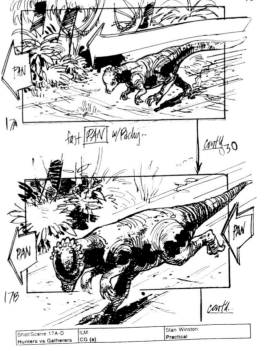

Shot/Scene:17A-D | ILM: | Stan Winston:
Hunters vs Gatherers | CG (a) | Practical

This page and opposite:
Background plates were first filmed on location with actors. Then ILM created digital storyboards as they began the process of creating and incorporating the CG dinosaurs. Here, storyboard illustrations, ILM's digital storyboards, and the final ILM composite shot.

ILM digital storyboards, and the final composite shots of the stegosaurus herd.

happen until we got there on the set and Steven made his decisions. We didn't know how many vehicles would be in any given shot, for example, or how much space they would cover in the course of a shot."

By the third week, Spielberg and the production crew had more than hit their stride. The final week was slated for the filming of the stegosaur sequence, for which both Winston's full-size adult stegosaur and the baby had been transported to the Prairie Creek site. "There were concerns about us bringing hydraulic characters into a protected state

park," Alan Scott noted, "but we went to great pains to ensure there would be no hydraulic leaks. And even if there were, we had all of the materials on hand for cleaning it up immediately." The updated hydraulic and telemetry operation of the stegosaurs mandated only a small puppeteering crew to achieve a complex and fully realized performance.

Working with the baby stegosaur was one of the highlights of the shoot for Julianne Moore. "It was such a beautiful animal," Moore said. "I told Stan at the time how beautiful she was, and how easy he had made my job in those scenes. As

Right: Sarah's encounter with the baby stegosaurus. *Below, left:* Dave Grasso of the Stan Winston Studios preps the baby stegosaurus for shooting.

Right: Areas within the state parks were carefully dressed with real and synthetic trees, plants, and logs. Stand-by painter Tony Leonardi paints a synthetic hollow log in preparation for filming. *Middle, right:* In the film, Sarah hides in the log to escape an enraged stegosaurus.

actors, we have to endow things all the time with some kind of personality or life; but I didn't have to do any work at all with the baby stegosaur. I mean, there she was—completely present and alive! I think Stan was very pleased that I felt that way about it, because that's what he strives for. He gave all of these animals so much life and personality—I loved working with them."

In the end, only the baby stegosaur scenes were filmed on location, while scheduled shots of the adult's attack on

Sarah were postponed and rescheduled for filming onstage at Universal Studios. Once on location, Spielberg, Winston, and stunt coordinator Gary Hymes had agreed that the potentially dangerous stunts involving the full-size rig—particularly the massive spiked tail—could be orchestrated more safely in the controlled environment of a sound stage.

Wider shots of the male stegosaur chasing Sarah through the forest and the small herd in a stream bed were slated for the digital team. On the shooting schedule for September 17 was a crane shot showing Sarah running through the stream bed and into a hollow log, with the stegosaur running close behind. Effects liaison Michael Fallavollita had come to the shoot prepared with "monster sticks"—twenty-five to thirty-five-foot poles used to guide the actors' eyelines in the CG effects scenes. A monster stick representing the stegosaur was positioned at the site so that Dennis Muren

could determine the framing of the animal in the background. Camera and lighting crews also benefited from the device, since it served to demonstrate to everyone the height and position the CG dinosaur would occupy in any particular shot.

The physical effects crew was also involved in the background plate shoot, since the rampaging stego would be shaking trees as it roared through the stream bed. Timing was critical, since the CG animators would be tied to whatever environmental interaction was captured in the plates. Lantieri's crew consulted closely with Muren before rigging the interactive gags, then got to work tying back branches of synthetic trees that could be released at the appropriate moment. When everything was positioned and ready, Spielberg called for action and Julianne Moore began running down the stream bed. Moore's reactions to the invisible stegosaur and Lantieri's

Stan Winston with his crew on location in Prairie Creek State Park.

Above, left: The crew prepares for the stegosaurus scene in Prairie Creek State Park. An existing bridge was dubbed "stego bridge" because of its stego-like silhouette. *Above, right:* Throughout filming, "monster sticks" were used as stand-ins for the computer generated dinosaurs. Effects liaison Michael Fallavollita positions a pole for the filming of a stegosaurus scene.

timing in the release and shaking of the branches was orchestrated by Spielberg's voice shouting, "The stego's here! Now it's here! Go, go, go!" Moore ran, trees rumbled and shook, the camera crane boomed down on the action as Moore dove into the hollow log—and then Spielberg called "cut" and the whole thing was reset for another take.

"What was great about the stuff we shot for the CG stegosaurs in Eureka," Moore recalled, "was that Steven didn't leave me alone out there to figure out where the animals would be or what they were doing. As we were shooting, he'd be saying, 'Okay, here it comes; it's here now; there it is!' So it wasn't that difficult. It was just part of the job of acting. I actually enjoyed it, partly because of all the CGI guys, who were great. They'd come up to explain a scene to me, saying, 'Okay, there's a stego there, and over there is another one.' I was always teasing them about seeing things that weren't there."

Background plates for the stego crossing the stream had been photographed the previous Saturday and had required

similar interactive gags, with synthetic trees rigged to fall into the water as the animal crashed through. Fallavollita was positioned behind a log in the stream, where he made splashes to simulate the stego's foot interacting with the water. Additional water movement would be animated by the CG team in postproduction.

Despite such on-location manipulations, the production company took pains not to disrupt the natural environment. "When they were laying down track in the stream for the shot of Sarah running from the stegosaur," Dave Lowery recalled, "there was a five-foot-tall, vertical branch sticking out of a broken log in the river, and it was in the way of the track. You wouldn't think it was a big deal to move a single branch—but the rangers told us that there were some birds that liked to perch on that branch and pick fish out of the water. The rangers knew the park and the animals that well.

One of them carefully moved the branch to another log upstream so that the birds could catch their fish there. We kept our moving of things to a minimum because even little things like that had an impact on what went on in the park."

By the time the three-week Eureka shoot was over, all of the plates for ILM's three major CG sequences—the compy attack, the roundup, and the stegosaurus herd—and nearly half of the CG plates for the entire show, had been filmed. Within days those plates would be cut into scenes and delivered to ILM for the commencement of the computer animation task. The nearly immediate turnover of plates from the main unit to ILM was made possible by the fact that editor Michael Kahn, a longtime Spielberg collaborator, was at the location, cutting scenes as they were shot. "I'm usually there when Steven goes on location," Kahn explained. "We run the dailies right away, and I get his indications of how he'd like to cut the scene; and then I put it together, based on that information. Then we run it again and he

makes little amendments to the scene until we get it the way he wants it. We essentially edit as we go."

The plates would serve the upcoming CG assignment very well. "What I liked was that each of the sequences had a totally different look," Muren said, "which was remarkable considering all of those plates had been shot within a few miles of each other. The compy sequence filmed in Fern Canyon was cool and dark, with a lot of blue light; the roundup was bright and vast; and the stegosaurus plates were beautiful and lush green, with light streaming in between the trees. I was amazed at how different each location was, and how much those differences showed in the footage."

September 18, the last day of the location shoot, found the company in an area of the park called Cal Barrel. On the schedule was a shot of Kelly, Malcolm, and Eddie Carr on the high hide—a titanium cage raised to a height that would afford the characters safety and a clear view of the surroundings. "The high hides

Storyboards depicting a scene in which the characters inhabit a "high hide." Based on authentic field equipment, the high hide was a cagelike enclosure that could be raised to the level of the treeline and above, theoretically affording the characters safety.

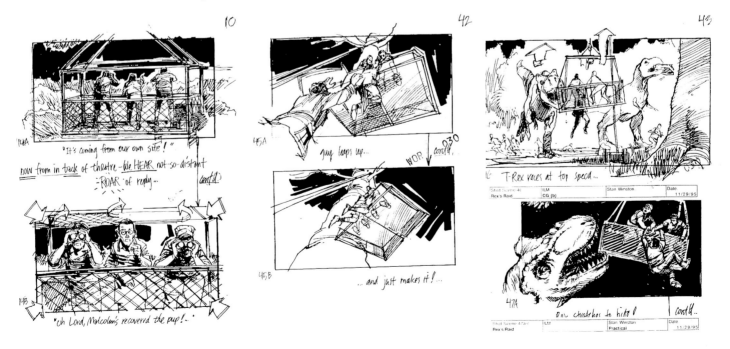

Below: Due to the difficult logistics of filming at such heights, most of the dialogue in the high hide scene was shot on a bluescreen stage, then composited into a wooded background. *Right:* For the few high hide shots that were captured on location, the actors were harnessed as a safety precaution.

were based on real equipment used by people that work in jungles to study animals," Lowery explained. "They build these raised platforms and live in the tree line so they'll be out of the way of nature. That way, the animals do what they do, without interference from the scientists, and they can study them from above." Built by Lantieri's crew from art depart-

ment designs, the high hides were erected to a height of fifteen feet on the forest floor at Cal Barrel. To establish the characters atop the platforms, the actors—wearing harnesses as a safety precau-

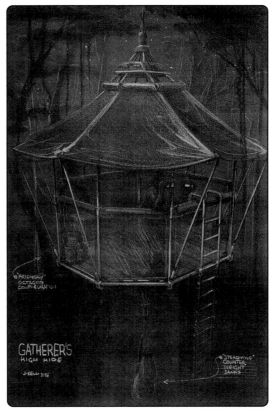

Initially, the production called for two versions of the high hide—one for the hunters and another for the gatherers. Storyline revisions made the hunter version unnecessary.

tion—were filmed briefly on the constructs; but the long dialogue scene on the high hide would be shot much later on a bluescreen stage at Universal.

The last day of shooting also captured shots of Sarah and Ian trekking through the forest. Many of the shooting days in Eureka had been at least partially devoted to such "wilderness trekking" shots. "It became kind of a joke," Julianne Moore said. "I'd arrive in the morning and ask, 'Okay, what are we doing today?' And they'd say, 'Marching. Marching. Marching some more. A lot of marching.' It was the kind of thing we wouldn't be able to do on stage, and we needed a lot of those shots."

On Thursday, September 19—three days ahead of schedule—the weary but satisfied crew boarded a chartered plane and left the quiet wonders of the redwood forest. Key live-action scenes had been

captured, dinosaurs were on film, and ILM had a good percentage of the plates they would need to start their computer animation of the CG dinosaurs.

But the shoot had been a resounding success in more ways than scheduling and the amount of spectacular footage in the can: the three weeks in Eureka had cemented relationships between all members of the cast and crew. "There was something about working in those beautiful quiet woods that was quite remarkable," Jeff Goldblum commented. "To come together and start a film in such magnificent surroundings was a very unifying experience. The whole company bonded there, in part because of the natural situation we were in. It was very nice to feel that kind of community, and it stayed with us throughout the production."

CHAPTER 7

FALL 1996:
UNIVERSAL STUDIOS

On Stage

A few days prior to the crew's departure, Rick Carter had returned to Los Angeles to prepare for the upcoming stage work, and to continue the hurried preparations for the new locations that would represent San Diego. "We only had about five or six weeks before we'd be shooting all of the San Diego scenes," Dave Lowery noted, "so Rick was out on the front lines of that, just as we were coming to an end of the work in Eureka. There were whole new locations to be found and prepped and new sets to be built."

Supervising art director Jim Teegarden had remained in Los Angeles throughout the Eureka shoot to spearhead construction of the Stage 27 set at Universal Studios, which would serve as the stage match to what had been shot at Patrick's Point for the T-rex-versus-the-trailer sequence. The stage was chosen both for its ample size and because it featured a large floor pit, used to simulate the drop for shots of the T-rex pushing the trailer toward the cliff's edge. "Based on photographs we'd taken at Patrick's Point," John Berger explained, "we built the silhouette of the real cliff edge there on stage. So the drop on stage had the same outline as the drop at Patrick's Point, with Wedding Rock to the right and the actual point to the left." Some adjustments were made to the Stage 27 set to accommodate

changes made to the Patrick's Point location during filming. "We took more photographs after we'd put the trailer there and dressed it with our foam logs, so that Jim Teegarden could see what we had done up there and dress the stage set accordingly."

Most of what was shot on Stage 27 involved the characters' points of view from inside the trailer as it approaches the cliff's edge, as well as shots of them hanging by ropes after the trailer has fallen and crashed below. Michael Lantieri was responsible for rigging the full-size trailer gags onstage. "We used winches and cables to drag the trailer onstage," Lantieri said, "as if the T-rex was pushing it, and we used hydraulics to actually jackknife it off the side of the floor pit. Hydraulics were also rigged inside the trailer to make the whole thing jump off the ground, as if

Opposite: An enraged T-rex demolishes Eddie Carr's vehicle during the pivotal "T-rex-versus-the-trailer" scene. *Below:* Eddie Carr's attempt to rescue Ian, Sarah, and Nick.

it were being impacted by the rex. What made it especially difficult was that this entire scene was supposed to be taking place in the rain, so we had the rain going onstage the whole time."

The rigors of the scene and the continuous stage rainfall made the two-week-long Stage 27 shoot one of the most uncomfortable periods of the schedule for the actors. "Those trailer scenes were the most difficult of the show for Vince and Jeff and me," Julianne Moore commented. "We were hanging upside down in harnesses, and they had the rain going onstage, soaking us. It was freezing onstage too. They couldn't raise the temperature because if it got too warm, the water would form condensation on all the camera lenses. On top of that, we were all bunched together and tangled up—Jeff said we looked like a string of peppers and garlic hanging over a stove. Every day, we would get to a point where we just couldn't hold it in anymore, and we'd crack up. And then there would be times when we got very quiet, just shaking and shivering from the cold. It was hellish.

Fortunately, Steven worked as quickly as possible so that we could get it over with. He'd set something up, we'd shoot it, and he'd say, 'Okay, we've got that one. Let's go on.'"

For specific interactive shots, the trailer would also be set up on Stage 24, where Winston's hydraulic T-rexes had been mounted on dolly track. Stage 24 was where all of the physical interaction with the mechanical T-rexes would take place, whether it was at the gatherers' camp, the hunters' camp, or at the San Diego settings. "Rather than move the T-rexes from stage to stage and set to set," Colin Wilson explained, "we decided to move the sets around the T-rexes. These things weighed nearly eighteen thousand pounds apiece; so they were a lot of trouble to move, and it took a long time to get them set up and working. It made more sense to build the sets around them." Rick Carter had observed that the plan to revolve the sets around the hydraulic rigs made the T-rexes the ultimate spoiled movie stars—they didn't go to the set, the set came to them.

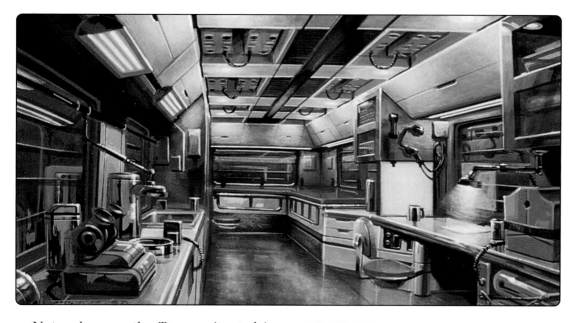

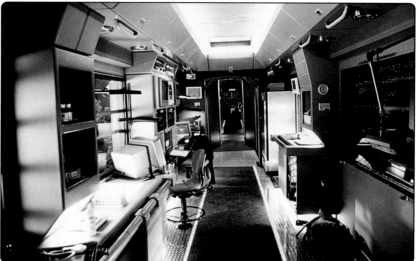

Left: Sean Hargreaves' painting of the trailer interior. *Below:* The actual trailer interior. The T-rex-versus-the-trailer scene was such a complex sequence, it was broken down into small bits that were filmed on location or on stages rigged by Michael Lantieri.

Not only were the T-rexes situated in one stage—their positions on that stage had been set in stone when the dolly track on which they would be mounted had been laid. "There was an eighty-foot-long track," Berger explained, "and once that was set, everything had to be built around that specific positioning. There was also a T-section of track running off the main track, which allowed for the rexes to come in at an angle."

Just as he had done for the first film, Michael Lantieri collaborated with the Winston team in mounting the massive T-rex rigs onstage. "We had to open up the stage floors to lay the track down," Lantieri said, "and then anchor it securely. Because of the force of the hydraulic T-rexes, we had engineers come in and consult with us on the anchoring designs. When the rex moved his head from right to left at full speed, he could pull two g's of force—enough to tear the track right out of the ground. It was the equivalent to the g-force of a fighter plane. The rexes this time around were more mobile and much quicker—and that meant they could do a lot more damage."

The T-rex-versus-the-trailer scenes shot on Stage 24 represented Jeff Goldblum's first major head-to-head contact with the Winston dinosaurs for *The Lost World*. "On the first movie," Goldblum noted, "the technology involved with Stan's dinosaurs hadn't interfered very much with what we were doing onstage. It was fast and they had it down really well. But this time, it was even faster and smoother. The dinosaurs were more sophisticated and their performance abilities were really upgraded—they were amazing and

Storyboards illustrate the pivotal T-rex-versus-the-trailer sequence.

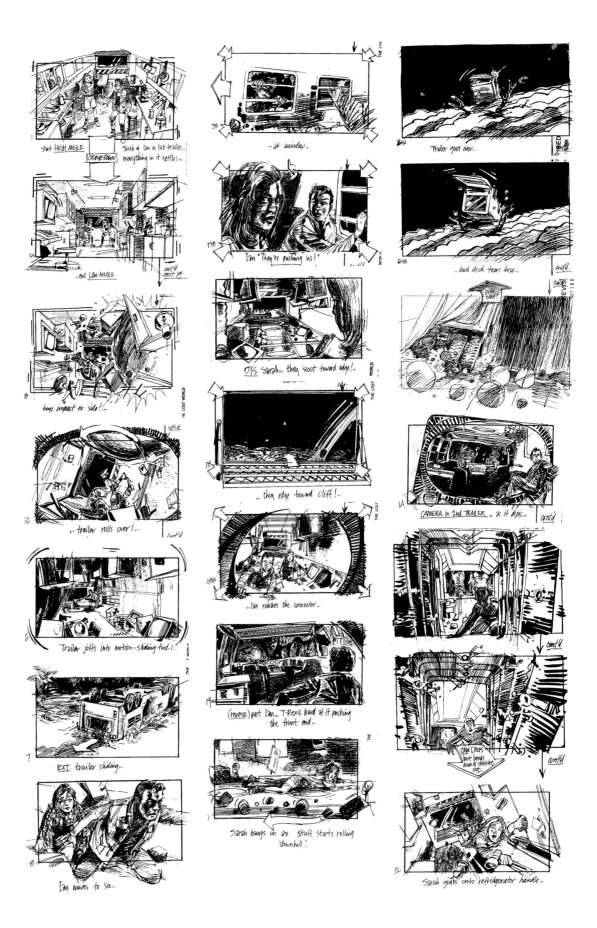

real and completely lifelike. It was a wonderful thing to act against."

Julianne Moore found the experience of working with the full-size rexes to be appropriately terrifying. "They were really scary. We'd been warned that they were potentially dangerous. We had these safety meetings, and they'd tell us, 'These animals weigh eighteen thousand pounds apiece—*do not go near them.*' And everybody listened." The full power of the hydraulic rexes was demonstrated one day as the crew filmed shots of Goldblum, Moore, and the baby T-rex inside the trailer, with the male and female rexes swinging their heads back and forth on either side. "One of the mechanical heads got a little close to the trailer and actually hit it. I screamed bloody murder! It made a huge dent in the trailer—that's how massive these things were."

In addition to the location footage filmed at Patrick's Point and the shots captured on Stages 27 and 24, the T-rex-versus-the-trailer sequence would require special setups on Stage 22—where the trailer would be mounted to a gimbal to facilitate vertical, dangling shots—and on Stage 23, where another rig would make it possible to roll the trailer 360 degrees. Night exteriors of the trailer hanging over the cliff were filmed atop a multistory parking structure at Universal Studios.

Much of the action took place on Stage 27, where laid track and a deep pit facilitated shots of the animal pushing the trailer over a cliff.

The T-rex-versus-the-trailer shoot on Stage 27. A complex system of weights, pulleys, winches, and levers was devised to realize the trailer's slide and ultimate descent.

Below: For closeups, the actors were suspended from the trailer in safety harnesses.

"We'd talked about building a fifty-foot wall out in the middle of the backlot," Pete Tobyansen said, "and I said, 'How are we going to access the top of this wall?' Someone suggested we could put in levels leading to the top. I said, 'Sounds like a parking garage to me—and we have one, right there!' We dressed the side of the building to look like a cliff, and just hung the trailer over the side—which was a big job for Michael Lantieri." Lantieri duplicated the winch and cable rigging he had set up on stage for the parking structure gag, which took a full two nights to film.

In addition to shooting the different setups for the T-rex-versus-the-trailer sequence, the company spent much of the month of October filming scenes on the hunters' camp set on Stage 12, which was then reconfigured and redressed for the rex raid on the combined hunter/gatherer campsite. Most of the T-

rex shots in the raid would be computer generated; however, for specific insert shots of the mechanical rex, parts of the Stage 12 set were re-created on Stage 24. "For the rex raid sequence," Lantieri recalled, "we had the rex chew the top off of a Mercedes AAV, chew through the door, and bite through the windshield— and we did it all with Stan's T-rex. It was incredible—a full-size, live, mechanical rex biting through the roof of a car, tearing it off, and almost lifting the car off the ground."

Following shots of the group running from the T-rex were filmed on an extensive ravine set on Stage 28. To create a sense of the great outdoors, the height of the set would be extended digitally, with ILM compositing matte paintings to mask

Above: Shots featuring the mechanical T-rexes were filmed on Stage 24. The Winston crew creates a T-rex performance by puppeteering the off-camera telemetry controls. *Above, left:* The T-rex-versus-the-trailer sequence is initiated when Sarah and Nick take the baby T-rex into the mobile unit in order to mend its broken leg. *Near left:* Looking for its baby, the T-rex approaches the trailer. *Far left:* Nick and Sarah tend to the baby T-rex.

Top: Eddie's attempt to secure the slipping trailer is aborted by a deadly confrontation with the T-rex. *Right and below:* The T-rex and trailer setup on Stage 24.

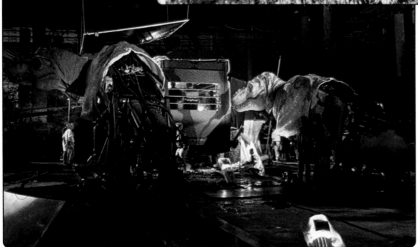

the sound stage ceiling. Stage 28 was also the site of the T-rex nest, where Roland and Ajay first discover the baby T-rex. The set—charged to assistant art director Stefan Dechant—featured a nest within a large cave, where a parasaurolophus carcass lies rotting. During filming, Spielberg reminded actors Pete Postlethwaite and Harvey Jason to wave their hands upon entering the cave. When Postlethwaite inquired as to why, Spielberg replied,

"Flies. You have to wave the flies away."

"But there aren't any flies," Postlethwaite protested. "Won't we look silly waving our hands in the air?"

"You'll look silly if you don't," Spielberg informed him, "because ILM is putting CG flies into the scene."

Sarah, Malcolm, and Nick's release of the caged dinosaurs and sabotage of the hunters' camp—as well as the chaos that follows as the animals destroy the campsite—was filmed late in October at the Los Angeles County Arboretum, a horticultural preserve and research center encompassing 127 acres of trees and shrubs. There, Lantieri executed large-scale effects

Top: Ian, Nick, and Sarah brace themselves as the trailer rolls toward the cliff. *Middle:* Sarah is slammed against a window during the attack. *Left:* Some views of the falling trailer were filmed from the side of a parking structure. Stunt doubles hang from the parking structure trailer.

Right: Although most of the hunters' camp scenes were filmed on a set on Stage 12, shots of the camp's destruction after the caged dinosaurs are freed were achieved at the Los Angeles Arboretum. The fiery scene entailed numerous large-scale effects gags. *Below:* Sarah, Nick, and Ian find a variety of herbivores caged at the hunters' base camp. Here, a concept drawing of a caged triceratops by Sean Hargreaves.

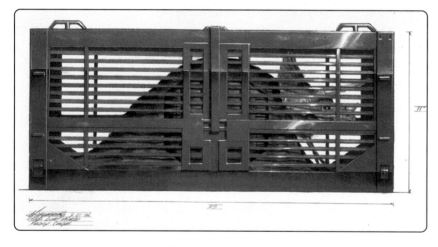

tured a practical effect of a triceratops running beneath a tent canvas. Winston crew members Paul Romer, Tim Nordella, and Lloyd Ball had mechanized a triceratops shape from the neck to the top of the head; that form was then mounted to a running cart rig devised by Lantieri. A brief shot of the triceratops emerging from beneath the tent would be computer animated.

Principal photography continued on the backlot laboratory compound set, where night scenes featuring Malcolm, Sarah, Kelly, and Nick fending off raptors as they wait for the arrival of a rescue helicopter were filmed. In an effort to make the Southern California terrain match the lushness of the northern coast, the sprawling set had been surrounded by literally hundreds of plants and trees by the greens crew. "We put in about ninety thirty-five-foot eucalyptus trees," greensman Kevin Mangan said, "dozens of synthetic, fiberglass palm trunks with real palm fronds at the top, plus a few hun-

for the chaos scene—knocking over vehicles, as if impacted by raging animals, and setting fire to the campsite. "We blew up six vehicles at the arboretum," Lantieri recalled, "as well as flipping a Humvee and catapulting another Humvee that's hit by the triceratops and flies forty feet in the air, landing in a tree."

The Stan Winston Studio provided the caged animals for the scene, while full-motion animals would be computer animated. The destruction scene also fea-

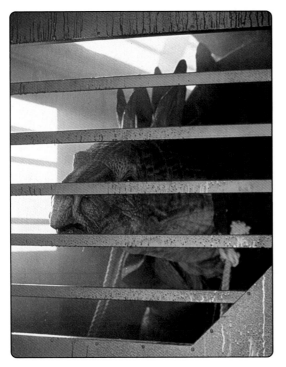

A caged adult stegosaurus and adult triceratops. Both creatures were built and operated by the Winston crew.

dred miscellaneous potted trees, in everything from five-gallon containers to three-foot boxes for some of the larger trees."

Filming on the set included the party's trek through the dinosaur graveyard, the subsequent discovery of the compound, and the arrival and takeoff of the rescue helicopter from the laboratory roof. Most of the days-long backlot shoot, however, was committed to filming the action-packed raptor chase, which would be accomplished with both CG shots and Winston's mechanical rigs. "The mechanical raptors seemed totally real," said Jeff Goldblum, who spent much of his time on the set dodging raptors, both real and imagined, "but it was also fun to do the CG scenes, where the raptors weren't actually there on the set. It was a bit more challenging to act against invisible raptors than it had been to act against an invisible T-rex, because they move so incredibly fast. I had to keep track of where they were at all times as they were

supposedly jumping around from here to there. It was really a challenge."

The night of October 31 was an especially CG effects-heavy one, with Julianne Moore performing many of her most interactive scenes with the raptors. "There were a lot of raptor pounces on Sarah that night," animation director Randy Dutra recalled. "There was cable on her to jerk her back, as if she were being impacted by the animal—so there were a lot of timing issues." One shot called for Moore to be knocked down by a raptor that has leapt from the top of a car twelve feet away. "They wanted to show the leap and the raptor's impact with Sarah all in one shot, without cutting away, so that we would see the brute force of these animals." In addition to the interaction with Moore, Michael Lantieri had arranged for set pieces and other props to be moved around, as if being knocked over by the raptors. "That kind of thing on the set gave us wonderful things to key off of in the animation," Dutra noted, "and it made such a difference in the final shot."

CHAPTER 8

NOVEMBER 1996:
LOS ANGELES

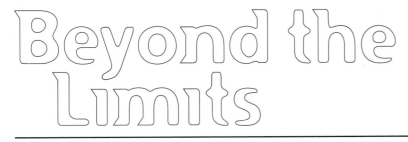

Beyond the Limits

On November 7 and 8, crew and equipment were transported to rural Newhall, fifty miles north of Los Angeles, for the filming of the "raptors in the grass" sequence. Michael Lantieri's crew had been responsible for growing the eight acres of elephant grass in Newhall, an agricultural project initiated the previous summer to ensure the grass would reach the required five-foot height in time for the scheduled filming of the scene.

After several nights of shooting in atypically cold weather, the crew in Newhall was visibly uplifted by the warm breezes that softly rustled through the grass. Under the movie lights the fields looked almost neon green, and the con-

trast of color against the total blackness of the rural sky gave the location a surreal quality that was only heightened when clouds of mist rose from strategically positioned fog machines.

The actors called for the night included Jeff Goldblum, Julianne Moore, Vince Vaughn, and Harvey Jason, in addition to about a dozen extras playing survivors of the InGen hunting party. All of the actors spent the best part of the evening running through the tall grass as Spielberg captured footage for the raptor assault scene. "Both Jeff Goldblum and Vince Vaughn are well over six feet tall," Moore commented, "and I'm five feet, five inches tall. So we'd all start running, and these guys didn't pull back for me at all. Steven

Opposite: A suspenseful scene, in which raptors chase expedition members through a field of tall grass, was shot in a rural location north of Los Angeles and employed several of the mechanical raptor rigs. *Below:* Sean Hargreaves' concept painting of the scene.

would be shouting, 'Faster! Faster!' And they'd run even faster, and I'd be farther and farther behind. I'd hear Steven's voice yelling, 'C'mon, Julianne! You're not running fast enough!' And I'd yell back, 'I'm running as fast as I can!' It got to be funny."

Stan Winston's crew was there with both hydraulic and insert head versions of the raptors, which are first revealed in the scene as three predatory heads rise, one at a time, from the grass. To heighten the suspense, the raptors would be hidden in the grass throughout much of the chase, with only an occasional appearance of a head or tail. Winston puppeteers—armed with flexible, springy raptor tails—crouched in the field, holding tightly to the appendages below the grass line. On Spielberg's command—a nontechnical, but effective "Okay, go!"—the puppeteers released the tails, maneuvering them from below to sway ominously above the field.

Mechanical raptors were mounted onto bobsleds to achieve the effect of the lightning-fast animals running through the grass. "We strung pulleys and cables out in the field so that we could pull these bobsleds with the raptors mounted on them," Lantieri said. "If they were working with the insert raptor heads, the puppeteers would ride on the bobsleds as well. When they were using the fully hydraulic raptors, the puppeteers could operate them remotely, from off-camera. In either case, we slid these sleds along the ground, to make it look as if the raptors were speeding through the grass."

Dennis Muren was at the Newhall site to film plates for a wide, high view of the characters running toward camera, followed by quickly lengthening trails as the raptors close in. Inspired by similar images of advancing torpedoes in innumerable World War II movies, the "torpedo shot" was the most crucial of the sequence in Steven Spielberg's mind. In fact, the director had determined early on that if that one shot could not be accomplished, the raptors in the grass sequence would be dropped. "It was difficult to find just the right setup to do this shot," Muren recalled. "The best situation

Sean Hargreaves' rendering of the "raptors in the grass" scene.

would have been to find grass that would pop back up after it had been pushed down by the raptor bobsleds, so that they could shoot additional takes. But they couldn't find grass that would do that. They ended up growing grass in four quadrants. After shooting in one quadrant, they couldn't shoot in it again, because once the grass was stomped down, that was it. So they'd move on to another quadrant, and so on."

To get the torpedo trail shots, Lantieri's crew had initially attempted to mow the grass down by way of the raptor/bobsled rigs. But Spielberg was unsatisfied with the look and speed of the practical effect, and a digital plan was hatched. "We shot the virgin grass before anything had trampled it down," Muren explained. "Then, without the camera rolling, we cut these paths in the grass. So we wound up with two plates—one with no trail in it,

and another with the entire trail, from beginning to end, already formed in the grass. In postproduction we would do a wipe from one plate to the other, revealing the trails at exactly the speed we wanted, and adding the CG raptors so it would look as if the animals were running at great speed."

November 11 and 12 found the company at the Media Center in Burbank, a once depressed downtown area that in recent years had been rejuvenated with new construction and a lot of civic dollars. Now, it was a thriving entertainment

Below, left: The survivors march through the five-foot-tall grass. Eight acres of elephant grass were cultivated by the special effects team months prior to filming. *Below, right:* The crew prepares for a crane shot of the raptors in the grass. *Bottom, left:* A mechanical raptor rig is positioned in the field. *Bottom, right:* Cast and crew ready themselves for filming.

Near right: Ajay prepares for death as a raptor advances. *Far right:* The raptors were puppeteered by remote, their heads popping up from the tall grass on Spielberg's command. *Below:* A Winston crew member touches up a raptor just prior to filming.

center with shops, department stores, restaurants, and movie theater screens. Curiosity was evident in the drivers who slowed their cars past the cordoned-off area, but none of the onlookers imagined what efforts had gone into securing the site for the filming of the T-rex's rampage through the streets of San Diego.

The shoot date had grown alarmingly near before the Burbank location was pinned down. Assistant location manager

Alex Reid had been partially responsible for finding a suitable location for the street scenes, and his search had started in San Diego, where, in concert with Rick Carter, he had canvassed the Gaslamp Quarter of the city's old town area. San Diego had been abandoned, however, when Spielberg and his producers decided to settle for a location nearer to Los Angeles rather than transporting cast, crew, and equipment to a city located nearly two hours to the south. San Diego would still be filmed for establishing shots of the downtown skyline and the harbor—but the committing of those few shots to film would amount to only a small, two-day, second-unit shoot.

The plan to shoot the San Diego street scenes locally was confirmed a scant sixteen days before their filming was scheduled. Even then, the exact locale remained undecided. "We looked at a couple of different areas," Reid said, "but when we found the Media Center, both Steven and Rick thought that it had just

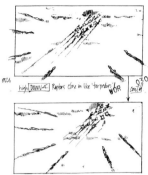

Above: Storyboard sketches.
Left: Final ILM composite of the raptor attack.
Below: For a San Diego street scene involving the escaped T-rex, a bus was rigged to crash into a Blockbuster Video set built on an empty lot in Burbank.

the look they were after. So we went to the city of Burbank to see if they were open to us filming here." In previous years, Burbank had tended to shun movie production within its city limits; but that attitude had begun to change, and city officials were delighted at the prospect of hosting a new, extravagant film by Steven Spielberg—although their approval was contingent upon the consent of the nearly seventy-five merchants who would be most affected by the production.

After determining what stretch of the Media Center would be needed, Reid and his crew spent two weeks going door-to-door, talking with the merchants and businesses that would have to be shut down for filming. "We talked to all seventy-five stores and establishments," Reid said, "all the way from the 'mom and pop' newsstand to the bigger name franchises, and they were all very open to it. They could see the income it would generate and the interest it would bring to the area."

In the hours leading up to the Media Center night shoot, all of the establishments were closed, and electricians and grips arrived to rig the designated five-block-long filming area—three blocks for filming, plus an additional block on either end to accommodate trailers and equipment. As part of the prep, street signs within the filming area were

changed to reflect actual San Diego streets: "Orange Grove" and "Palm" became "Beach" and "Cedar," and the main thoroughfare itself, "San Fernando Boulevard," was changed to "Balboa." The set dressing department also made some modifications to storefronts— mainly to avoid revealing establishments in direct competition with companies that had arranged promotional tie-ins

Near right: At Burbank's Media Center, Spielberg oversees film preparations from the top of a camera truck. *Far right:* Spielberg, with director of photography Janusz Kaminski below. *Below:* Extras portrayed pedestrians being chased down a street by the T-rex. *Below, right:* The crew watches a run-through of the scene. *Bottom, left:* To simulate the rex's impact, Lantieri rigged a bus to buckle on cue. *Bottom, right:* The camera shoots the bus head-on.

with the movie. "We did some creative set dressing, turning off some signs, covering up logos that were too recognizable—that kind of thing," Reid said.

Filming started at approximately 6 P.M. First up was a big mechanical effect for a CG scene in which the T-rex chases and then rams a moving city bus. "Steven wanted it to look as if the rex threw his shoulder into the bus," Lantieri said, "making a huge dent in the side. To do that, we prepared the walls on the inside of the real bus so that we could essentially collapse them with super high-pressure pneumatics. We also attached cables to the walls so we could pull them in at the moment of impact." Additional effects preparation included replacing the bus windows with breakaway glass and setting charges that would blow open the bus doors. "We also rigged the bus with hydraulics to make the wheels come off the ground on the side that would be hit by the rex. To keep it from tipping all the way over, we had some safety rigs on the off-camera side, which would be painted out digitally by ILM." More mayhem was created with mechanical slides in the bus interior, rigged to catapult stunt passengers out of the breakaway windows.

The rex encounter with the bus wasn't just a matter of large-scale, bull-in-a-china-shop type of mechanical rigging, however. It also required exquisite precision and a keen sense of timing. "All of this had to be set and choreographed to happen right on cue—and, of course, without the rex present," Lantieri commented. "We had to figure out how fast the rex would be running, what part of the rex would hit the bus and at what spot on the bus the most damage would occur, where the rex was at all times and how fast the bus was traveling when it

was hit." With the assault by the T-rex, the bus loses control and proceeds to crash into a Blockbuster Video storefront. Shots leading up to the crash were filmed at the Media Center location, while interior views and the actual bus impact would be executed as an effects setup on stage.

Also on the agenda for the night were shots of fifty-some people streaming out of a nightclub, then running for their lives as the T-rex advances down the street—an obvious and wholly intentional nod to the high-camp *Godzilla* movies of the fifties. "I've waited my whole life to do a *Godzilla* movie," Spielberg joked as he watched the scene on his monitor, "and this is it." Having determined that comparisons to the cheesy Japanese pictures would be inevitable, Koepp and Spielberg had decided to acknowledge the comparison first. Thus, one of the prominent characters in the fleeing crowd is a Japanese businessman who looks back over his shoulder at the approaching T-rex and says—in Japanese—"I left Tokyo to get away from this!"

The crowd of extras—followed by a

Top: Spielberg and key production personnel on location at the Media Center. *Above:* The Media Center shoot included a cameo by screenwriter David Koepp, who portrayed one of the T-rex's victims.

Above: For fun, Spielberg allowed crew members to act as pedestrians being chased by the T-rex. *Right:* Spielberg on location in Burbank.

camera car with a T-rex-size monster stick to guide their eye lines—ran through the drill a number of times before Spielberg got a satisfactory take. Included in their numbers was David Koepp, who had written a small cameo part for himself—the "Unlucky Bastard" who breaks off from the running crowd and attempts to find shelter in a bookstore, banging desperately at the locked glass door before the T-rex picks him up in his powerful jaws and consumes him. "When I was writing this

scene," Koepp said, "I decided that if people were going to get eaten by the T-rex, I wanted to be one of them. I asked Steven if I could do it, and he said: 'Kill you on film? No problem!' I'd never done anything like this before, but I thought this was one role I couldn't screw up too badly. It was screaming and running; and I thought: 'I can scream. I can run. How hard could it be?'" Dressed in nondescript brown pants and a flannel shirt, Koepp waited for his moment in front of the camera, sitting near Spielberg in his usual director's chair—on which the silk-screened "David Koepp" had been taped over to read "Unlucky Bastard" for the night. "It was great fun to do it, but it was harder than I had expected. It was surprisingly difficult to react to something that wasn't there—to pretend to be yanked back from the door and then eaten by a nonexistent dinosaur." When his scene wrapped hours later, Koepp's performance earned enthusiastic applause from the entire crew.

The Media Center shoot went exceedingly well; and everyone was in good spirits on the second night at the location. The evening was so fruitful and the mood so light, in fact, that after Spielberg had shot his final take of the running crowd, director of photography Janusz Kaminski, egged on by Kathy Kennedy, suggested they shoot one more take of the crowd—but this time, the screaming mass would be made up entirely of crew members. With the air of an indulgent parent, Spielberg said, "Oh, all right—go ahead. But when I yell 'Cut,' don't keep going. Please come back." At "Action" all one hundred or so members of the crew—including Kaminski, producer Colin Wilson, Dennis Muren, and executive producer Kathy Kennedy—were filmed running and screaming down the street, a rare moment of frivolity in the serious and often grueling ordeal of making a movie.

Following nights found the company in Granada Hills, a valley suburb where shots of a Union 76 gas station ball rolling down a street, past Sarah and Malcolm in a car, were filmed. A suburban house in the Granada Hills neighborhood was also pegged for the exteriors of Ben's house, where the rex would wander into the backyard and past the little boy's window to drink from the family pool. Interiors of Ben's bedroom were filmed the following week, on sets erected on Stage 24. Because the T-rex rig was mounted to a dolly in the stage floor and could only move forward at one particular angle, two bedroom sets on platforms had been constructed at right angles. One set was used for shots of the T-rex walking past the window in profile, while the second set facilitated shots of the T-rex approaching the window head on.

On November 18, after filming Ben's bedroom scenes all morning, the crew broke for lunch to enjoy the crew Thanksgiving potluck, organized by makeup supervisor Christina Smith and costume supervisor Sue Moore, and set up on Stage 23. Dishes such as "Ajay Pâté," "Chili Raptor Relleno," and "Compy Tails" (green beans) were laid out on sound stage tables.

Among those attending was Vanessa Lee Chester, who had just recently completed her last scene for *The Lost World*, after spending most of the preceding three months working for the most celebrated director of child actors in film history. "I loved working with Steven," Chester said. "When I thought about *why* I loved working with him so much, the thing that came to mind was his voice. I love his voice, the way it sounds. I tried to explain that to my mom while we were still shooting—that Steven has the best voice in the world. And he would talk to me like I was a regular person, not a kid. He'd say, 'Hi, Vanessa, what's up?'—just like he'd say to Jeff or Julianne. I really

Crew members joined together on Stage 23 for a Thanksgiving buffet as *The Lost World* shoot wound down to the final weeks.

The production's last stop was Kauai, where the opening encounter between the little girl (Camilla Belle) and the compys was filmed, along with wide establishing shots of Isla Sorna.

liked that about him. But mostly I liked his voice."

After the Thanksgiving break, the company moved into one of the most difficult periods of the schedule—the six-day location shoot in San Pedro, where all of the exteriors for the San Diego dock sequences would be filmed. Located south of Los Angeles, the waterfront San Pedro area had yielded a marine ship rebuilding facility with a small harbor and pier. It was there that the company built both precrash and postcrash dock sets. The set representing the dock area after the ocean barge has crashed was dressed with cargo supposedly ejected in the impact of the ship, named the *SS Venture*.

One night of filming in San Pedro came to an abrupt end when thick, soupy fog rolled in. "Everyone was standing around on the dock," Julianne Moore recalled, "talking and getting ready for the next shot, and it started to get a little misty. Five minutes later you couldn't see a thing that was more than five feet in front of you. They said, 'Well, okay—I guess that's a wrap.'" After three nights in San Pedro, the crew broke for the four-day Thanksgiving holiday, then returned the following Monday for three more days of filming at the site.

At the end of November, Julianne Moore's scenes for *The Lost World* had been completed, and the inevitable ambivalence was there as she bade the production farewell. "The movie often felt like one long wilderness trek," Moore said, "even though we were on the lot throughout most of it. Every time I walked on stage, it seemed, it was raining, there was mud, someone was falling down. All of us were dirty for four months—absolutely filthy! It was all worth it, though, because I got to work with Steven. Aside from being just a wonderful guy, this is a man who is one of the great filmmakers, a man who is unparalleled as a director. Getting the opportunity to work with him was the end-all and be-all of this project for me."

All but a few scenes were now in the can, and the production was five days ahead of schedule. Remaining scenes included one in which John Hammond, confined to bed, urges Malcolm to join the Isla Sorna expedition. On the morning of Friday, December 6, a cold rain was

pouring as the company gathered at the Mayfair Catholic Girls' School in Pasadena to film the encounter. The Catholic school was on the grounds of what had once been a privately owned estate, an old but graceful manor sitting on a rolling green landscape near Pasadena's old town district. "It was a glorious house," Alex Reid noted. "It had very ornately carved wood, marble inlays, and floor-to-ceiling casement windows. The den was dressed as Hammond's bedroom and it was really beautiful. We knew it would have a very rich feeling on film."

The quiet dignity of the house, the presence of Lord Richard Attenborough, and the fact that school was in session all made for a subdued atmosphere throughout the day of filming. Crew members spoke in whispers when talking was necessary; and when it wasn't, they sat quietly in the elegant dining room adjacent to the den. Because the scene was a

Spielberg confers with Stan Winston on location in Hawaii.

In a brief scene at John Hammond's home, Ian reunites with the elderly man's grandchildren—Tim (Joseph Mazzello) and Alexis (Ariana Richards), characters first introduced in *Jurassic Park*.

particularly dialogue-intensive one—with five pages of the script devoted to Hammond's sickbed confession concerning Site B, and his urging of Malcolm to join his expedition there—David Koepp was on the set for the day. "I always tried to be there if they were shooting a difficult scene like that one," Koepp revealed. "Sure enough, Steven wanted some revisions, and I was there to do them. I also like to be on the set because I learn a lot from Steven—he is always in the mood to teach, and I am always in the mood to learn." Also there were Ariana Richards and Joseph Mazzello, the child stars of *Jurassic Park* for whom Koepp had written a brief scene.

At the first break in the quiet morning of filming, a last minute meeting between Spielberg and producers Colin Wilson, Jerry Molen, and Kathy Kennedy went into session. Now at the end of the shoot, and with a clearer picture of what he had been able to capture at both the Northern California and local locations, Spielberg was no longer convinced that a trip to New Zealand—a country that was literally on the other side of the world—was nec-

essary to complete his film. Both money and the even more precious commodity of time could be saved if the few remaining shots could be captured at a less remote location. Inevitably, the filmmakers' thoughts turned to Hawaii, where much of *Jurassic Park* had been filmed. By the time the impromptu meeting had ended, the decision had been made: production on *The Lost World* would finish up with four days of shooting on the island of Kauai.

The small crew in Hawaii included Spielberg, Jerry Molen, Kathy Kennedy, and David Koepp, who would be directing second unit photography there. "The second unit stuff amounted to shots of people marching across the island, some helicopter shots and other establishing views," Koepp explained. With Dennis Muren immersed in the CG effort at ILM, veteran effects supervisor Scott Farrar agreed to supervise the filming of the visual effects plates on the island, required for multiple compy shots in the opening scene. Stan Winston and a few members of his crew were also present on the island, their mission to extract a lifelike performance from a rod puppet for the encounter between the little girl and the compy. "It was the beginning of the film," Shane Mahan said, "and the first time a dinosaur would be seen in the movie—so it was a very critical shot. We had put a lot of thought into it before going, which paid off once we were on location."

When the Winston crew left Kauai toward the end of December, they were essentially closing the book on their *Lost World* assignment. The ultimate success or failure of their creature work was now in the hands of Steven Spielberg; but Winston harbored no concerns as to the

Open sea shots of the InGen barge were also shot in the waters off Hawaii.

way that work would be presented. "To some degree," Winston mused, "an artist is only as good as the standard he is held to; and never is an artist held to a higher standard than when working under the direction of someone like Steven Spielberg. I always think of that whenever effects get a lot of credit for the success of a movie—because the same artists can work on another film, with another director, and somehow the effects aren't as great. Ultimately, it all comes down to the director. Fortunately for us, Steven Spielberg is one of the greatest filmmakers of all time; and he knows how to use the

talent. We knew he would make our work on *The Lost World* look great."

Principal photography on *The Lost World* wrapped on December 20. For the majority of the main unit crews, the production was over. But in many respects, it was just beginning for the expanding team at Industrial Light & Magic. With all of the plates delivered and the footage cut into scenes, ILM launched into completing its slate of ninety computer-animated shots in time for a May 6 deadline—just three and a half weeks before the movie's scheduled release.

The race was on.

CHAPTER 9

JANUARY 1997:
SAN RAFAEL

Playing Music

With the wrap of principal photography, *The Lost World* entered its postproduction phase. Many tasks would have to be attended to during the following months. John Williams would write a score for the film, as he had its predecessor, and that score would have to be laid into the film, along with dinosaur sound effects being designed by Gary Rydstrom at Skywalker Sound.

But, essentially, the film was now in the hands of Industrial Light & Magic, where—for the next four and a half months—computer-animated dinosaurs and other visual effects, both CG and traditional, would be incorporated into

scenes that had been cut and finessed by Spielberg and editor Michael Kahn. The bulk of the editing chores had been completed just two weeks after the main unit had wrapped, since Spielberg and Kahn

Opposite: A final CG composite of Ian, Eddie, and Nick encountering a stegosaurus. Computer generated characters were animated and composited into background plates during a five-month postproduction period. *Above:* Composer John Williams on the scoring stage. *Left:* Dennis Muren confers with the crew at ILM as they build the miniature set that will depict the InGen dock in San Diego.

The talented staff at ILM hard at work. *Clockwise from left:* George Hull, Eric Jensen, Paul Huston, Lisa Smith, Lorne Peterson, Geoff Heron.

had been cutting the movie since the beginning of filming. "Through the shoot," Kahn explained, "Steven and I were adjusting scenes. So when he got back from Hawaii and I cut those scenes in, we were able to run the whole show together for the first time. We had our first cut of the movie within just a few days. At that point, Steven's only adjustments were to improve the totality of the movie and to make sure it worked as a whole. My job was almost over, except for laying in ILM's shots."

As they had for twenty-one years, Spielberg and Kahn cut the film the old-fashioned way—with real film and a Moviola—rather than rely on the elec-tronic wonders of a Lightworks or Avid digital editing bay, the method now used for the vast majority of films. "When it came time to cut *The Lost World*," Kahn recalled, "I asked Steven if he wanted me to use a Lightworks, and he said: 'No, no, no, you have to stay on film. I want to feel it. I want to touch it.' He's a traditionalist. He loves the history of film, and he doesn't want to lose the feeling that goes with that."

Because the film had been in the editing process from the first day of the shoot, plates had started arriving at ILM immediately after Dennis Muren and his crew returned from the initial three weeks of filming in Eureka. "We got the plates

The miniature ship crashes into InGen's dock. *Clockwise from left:* Keith London, Robert Edwards, Chris Reed, Randy Dutra, Danny Wagner.

Clockwise from left: Dave Hanks, Terry Chostner, Kevin Barnhill, Euan MacDonald, Amanda Ronai, Dan Taylor, Ken Bryan, George Aleco-Sima, Paul Giacoppo.

for the compy attack first," Ned Gorman recalled, "and started right in on that sequence. About two weeks later we started working on the roundup shots, the first of which was the head-butting of the truck. We had all of the stegosaur plates in by the end of October. What that meant was that we were doing some of our most difficult sequences right off the bat. All three—the compys, the roundup, and the stegosaurs—were multiple-creature shots; and those were the ones that we were having to reinvent the wheel for, since there'd been few of those

types of shots in the first movie."

Although specific advances had been made since the release of *Jurassic Park*, the general methodology for creating the computer generated dinosaurs had remained essentially the same. The first step was to build a computer model of each of the nine species that would be featured in the film. In most cases, those models were initiated by scanning maquettes provided by the Stan Winston Studio. The scan gave the ILM modelers the data from which a finessed model could be built. Animation was executed with the model still in wire-frame or partially rendered form. As the animation for

each shot was completed, technical directors dealt with the actual look of the character, creating appropriate lighting within the virtual realm so that the creature would look as if it had been filmed at the same time and under the same conditions as the live-action footage. Technical directors were also responsible for the application of realistic, organic-looking skin textures. Models were painted by artists working with ILM's proprietary painting program. To place the characters into a scene, each CG shot was match-moved and tracked to the plate, with all of the live-action camera moves precisely duplicated. After the computer-animated element was composited into the live-action, each shot was scanned back out onto film.

The naturalism required for *The Lost World* made for the most challenging of animation assignments. "This type of animation—naturalism—is one of the hardest things to do," animation director

Randy Dutra commented. "It is certainly the hardest thing to do convincingly, because the audience knows instinctively if something is an organic form or not, or if it is moving according to the laws of gravity. No matter how much you think you know about animation and animal behavior, animals always do the unexpected. They are spontaneous. No matter how good an animator is, he can never really duplicate the randomness you find in nature—but he can try."

Since all of the models had been built by the time principal photography on the

Top, left, clockwise from far left: Dan Taylor, Dennis Muren, Randy Dutra, Paul Giacoppo, Miguel Fuertes, Ben Snow. *Top, right:* Ken Nielsen, Ben Snow, Christina Hills. *Above:* Susan Ross.

film began in September, the animators had been able to segue into animation of specific shots as soon as the appropriate plates started to roll in. At its peak, the animation task would require the services of a twenty-five-member team, working under Dennis Muren, Randy Dutra, and animation leads Dan Taylor, Miguel Fuertes, Doug E. Smith, and Daniel Jeannette. "Dan Taylor was actually the only one of the four with a stop-motion background," Dutra commented, "but they were all wonderful animators, and they did a fantastic job." A team of thir-

Above: Production crew meeting. *Right and below, clockwise from left:* Dennis Muren, Ned Gorman, Eric Mattson, Michael Bauer, Kevin Rafferty, Susan Goldsmith, Jack Mongovan.

Among the first shots on ILM's CG slate were those in the stegosaurus sequence. Background plates shot in Eureka in September were edited and delivered to ILM by the first of October so that the animators and technical directors could begin work on the sequence immediately. The stegosaurs reveal themselves to Ian, Eddie, and Nick soon after their arrival on Isla Sorna.

teen technical directors would work in tandem with the animators, under the supervision of CG supervisors Euan Macdonald, Kevin Rafferty, and Ben Snow.

Of the three sequences the ILM team had immediately jumped into upon their return from Eureka, the roundup was the most ambitious. "It was not only the biggest sequence in terms of the number of animals," Muren stated, "it was also the biggest in that the vision of it was very broad and grand and bold. It had mixed scales of dinosaurs—with shots of

small dinosaurs running through the legs of the larger dinosaurs—and vehicles racing around and dust being blown up. The audience had seen the gallimimus stam-

From the beginning, Spielberg and Dennis Muren aimed to make the sequence as interactive as possible, with live-action characters coming into close contact with the CG creatures. Here are two ILM digital storyboards and the final composite shots.

pede in the first movie, but this stampede was much bigger and more varied and more interesting."

To simplify the animation of the large number of stampeding animals, the animation team had developed a library of running and walking cycles that could be "plugged in" as needed. In addition, software had been developed that would enable the animators to essentially draw a path through the live-action scene on

Because of the dynamic nature of its action, nearly every shot in the roundup sequence featured CG dinosaurs. *Above:* Steadicam operators film a background plate for a shot of the hunters rounding up a pachycephalosaurus. *Left:* The final shot with the CG herbivore incorporated. *Below:* Final shots of a CG pachycephalosaurus ramming one of the hunter vehicles. The herbivore is finally lassoed by a hunter. Both the pachy-cephalosaurus and the rope were computer generated.

their monitors for a specific CG character, and that character would automatically move along that course. After reviewing the shot, the animator could then adjust the animal's course simply by redrawing the path. The procedural approach was implemented for the

Final composites of the compy attack on Dieter. The sequence was realized with both mechanical compys and those generated digitally by ILM.

compy sequence as well, due to the large number of creatures in the scene.

To suggest the interaction of the hunters roping and bringing down a parasaurolophus during the roundup, a plate had been shot in Northern California, with extras as hunters holding on to ropes connected to a single fifteen-foot pole, moving and reacting as if trying to subdue the struggling animal. The intention was to computer animate the creature in such a way that its actions would correspond to the actions of the extras. "At one point," Gorman recalled, "Dennis said: 'You know, we're doing this backwards. What we need to do is shoot an empty plate of the background, then animate the parasaurolophus, and then shoot hunters on a bluescreen stage, staging their actions to what the animated parasaurolophus is doing.' And he was absolutely right. It was much better to have the animation of the character drive the scene than it was to slave the animation to what a bunch of extras had done on the set three months before."

The dynamic pace and action of the roundup scene was contrasted by the stegosaurus herd sequence, in which the slow-moving, tranquil animals are revealed in a stream. "There was a lot of subtlety that we managed to get into the stegosaurus performances," Muren said. "Those shots had a sense of history to them. For example, in one shot, a stegosaur walks into frame and shakes its head—as if it had been drinking *before* it walked into frame and was now shaking water off its neck. There is a sense of back story to that animal. Footage of real animals in the wild often have that same sense, and it's part of what makes them look real. You are looking at one captured moment. That moment may be right

The compy attack. Animation director Randy Dutra envisioned specific behaviors for each dinosaur species, such as the compys' ritualistic head-bobbing.

A major CG scene was one in which the T-rex raids the camp of the combined hunter-gatherer expeditions. Computer models for each dinosaur featured in the film were completed by the time filming wrapped in December 1996.

before the animal does something really neat and interesting, or right after the animal does something really neat and interesting. But it has a sense of something just captured, rather than something that has an orchestrating mind behind it. Little things like that add a texture of reality to the animation."

Shots delegated for later in the ILM schedule included those of the raptor chase in town. Although the raptors were not new characters for the digital team—

having played a major role in *Jurassic Park*—the chase sequence shots were particularly difficult because many would feature several interacting animals. "Even in the shots where the animals weren't fighting or interacting heavily with each other," Muren noted, "the animation was much more difficult just because there were multiple animals, and they all had to look absolutely real. The animation had to be just as detailed for each one of them, and there was no way to speed up that process. So those shots were harder, just because of the added volume of work. And then, in the shots where they interact, it was even more difficult. In one shot, we had two raptors fighting with each other, rolling around on the ground, and that was several times as hard."

The T-rex in San Diego was another major undertaking for the ILM crew. "That whole sequence was very perfor-

Digital storyboards from ILM depict a raptor chasing Ian through the worker village. *Below:* The final ILM composite.

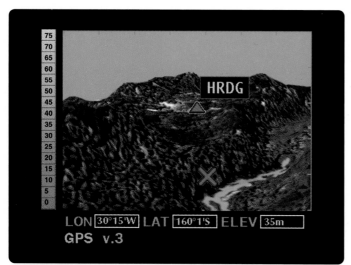

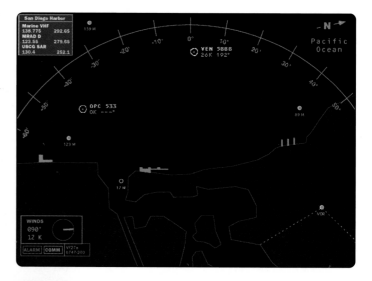

Dilophosaurus

Description: Skull has thin-walled double crest, large mouth with sharp teeth, light build, long and slender forelimbs, neck, and tail, 20 feet long

Todd Marks designed computer graphics displays for monitors inside the expedition's mobile lab.

mance oriented," Dutra noted, "because there was only one creature, standing out in this city environment. The focus was going to be entirely on the T-rex. It was also one of the more interactive sequences because the T-rex was ramming into a bus and grabbing people running in the street."

Other 3-D animation shots were scattered throughout the film: in the rex raid sequence, the T-rex-versus-the-trailer sequence, and the raptors in the grass

scene. Not all of the shots on ILM's slate were computer-animated dinosaurs, however. Computer models of the trailer and the Mercedes AAV were also built and animated in 3-D, as were some of the T-rex's kicking and screaming victims. Computer generated flies were incorporated into the T-rex nest scene—with a directive from Spielberg to make them "good and disgusting"—and digital matte paintings were rendered to extend stage sets.

In addition to the digital effects created for the film, ILM contributed a number of model photography shots, such as images of the InGen barge crashing into the dock in San Diego. An eighth-scale dock and ship miniature was built by model supervisor Warren Peterson and his crew, then shot on the ILM stages early in March. A counterweight pulley system was employed to drive the boat model through a balsa wood dock, and the resulting model photography was composited into background plates shot in San Pedro.

A miniature amphitheater stadium was also constructed and filmed for the sequence in which Malcolm and Sarah steal the baby T-rex from InGen's "Jurassic Park—San Diego" in order to

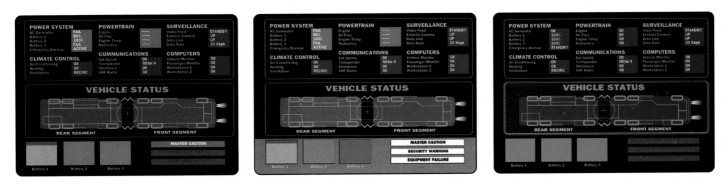

lure the rampaging T-rex back to the docked boat. Rather than build an entire stadium in full scale for the brief scene, Spielberg had shot the live-action with minimal set pieces, leaving the wide establishing shot of the amphitheater to the visual effects artisans. The stadium miniature was filmed, and the model photography was composited into the live-action footage.

ILM also provided the background for the dialogue scene within the high hide, which had been shot on stage, against a bluescreen. "The actual raising of the high hide had been shot on location," Gorman explained, "as was the shot of Malcolm getting out of the mesh basket at the top and sliding down the rope. But they didn't want to subject the actors to doing that entire dialogue scene in the high hide on location. By shooting it bluescreen, they had much more control over the lighting, and more control over the rain that was supposed to be falling— *and* they avoided the logistics of shooting the scene fifteen feet in the air, with harnessed actors on this thing." The blue-screen shoot provided isolated footage of the actors inside the high hide basket— but it existed in a blue limbo, without any surrounding environment. ILM photographed both real and half-scale trees for the background—manipulated to suggest interaction with a passing T-rex—and combined that photography with the

bluescreen elements. Computer generated rain was also added to enhance the scene.

When all ninety-one shots had been delivered just days prior to the movie's release, Muren was confident that he had met his own mandate: to play beautiful music on the Stradivarius that had been built for *Jurassic Park*. "At the start of *Jurassic Park*," Muren concluded, "I had many people say to me: 'How can you make dinosaurs that are any better than what you did for *Dragonslayer* with go-motion? Jim Danforth and other stop-motion animators have already done the most phenomenal animation possible— why are you attempting this? It can't be done any better than it already has been.' But then, *Jurassic Park* came out and it was clear that it *was* better than what had been done before.

"My hope for *The Lost World* was that the same thing would happen—that people who were thinking, 'It can't be done any better than *Jurassic Park*,' would see this movie and say, 'Yes—this is even better.'"

"Dennis used an expression that, I think, perfectly described our feeling at ILM about *The Lost World*," Ned Gorman added. "We didn't want this movie to be 'Side Two of the *Jurassic Park* album.' We wanted to take it so far beyond, that it would be its own record. And I think we did that. In our minds, *The Lost World* is the white album."

Graphics were also generated for displays in the gatherers' high-tech labtrailer.

CALL SHEET

UNIVERSAL PICTURES

Director: Steven Spielberg
Executive Producer: Steven Spielberg
Executive Producer: Kathleen Kennedy
Producers: Jerry Molen, Colin Wilson
Weather: Cloudy skies, slight chance of rain.
Temp 50-72, winds 5-10 mph
Sunrise: 6:12 AM **Sunset:** 5:01 PM
Script: Salmon 10/23/96

THE LOST WORLD — Jurassic Park

Day: Friday, November 1, 1996
43 Day out of **74**

CALL TIME: 5:00 PM
SHOOTING CALL: 6:30 PM

An aircraft will be used in today's filming activities, and be flown in close proximity to crew and equipment. Any talent or crew objecting to the above should notify the production manager or the 1st Assistant Director prior to any filming.

Universal Studios Backlot

SC / SB	Scene	Description	Pages	Cast
SC	144	EXT - HILLSIDE - NIGHT	1/8	1,2,3,5
SB		Group fall down the hillside.		1X,2X,3X,5X
SC	151 (pt.)	EXT - WORKER VILLAGE - GAS STATION - NIGHT	TBA	1
SB		Ian hides in jeep. Raptor breaks in thru glass.		1X RPT
SC	159	EXT - WORKER VILLAGE - MAIN STREET - NIGHT	3/8	1,2,3,5,25,32
SB		Group load aboard helicopter, rushed by InGen man, take off.		1X,2X,3X,5X
SC	158	EXT - WORKER VILLAGE - LAB - NIGHT	2/8	1,2,3
SB	100A-B	Sarah lands in street. Malcolm pulls her up. They hear helicopter.		2X
SC	156 (pt. 2 of 2)	EXT - KILN HOUSE ROOFTOP - NIGHT	1/8	2
SB	70, 83A-B,84	Sarah jumps roofs. Wide shot of her fighting the raptors.		2X
SC	154, 155A	EXT - KILN HOUSE (RAPTOR'S FEET) - NIGHT	2/8	RPT
SB	44	Raptor's feet digging the tunnel under the wall. Raptor crunches into pipe.		

TOTAL PAGES 3 7/8

No smoking on set!
No forced calls without prior approval of D. Scott Easton.
Non-deductible (ND) breakfast is provided for all early calls.
All calls subject to change by assistant directors.

CAST & DAY PLAYERS	STATUS	CHARACTER	LEAVE	MU/HAIR/WARDROBE	SET CALL	REMARKS
Jeff Goldblum	W	1. Ian Malcolm		5:00 PM	5:00 PM	REPORT TO BACKLOT
Julianne Moore	W	2. Sarah Harding		5:00 PM	6:00 PM	REPORT TO BACKLOT
Vanessa Lee Chester (K-12)	W	3. Kelly		5:30 PM	6:00 PM	REPORT TO BACKLOT
Richard Schiff	H	4. Eddie Carr		Hold		
Vince Vaughn	H	5. Nick Van Owen		5:00 PM	6:00 PM	REPORT TO BACKLOT
Arliss Howard	H	6. Peter Ludlow		Hold		
Pete Postlethwaite	H	7. Roland Tembo		Hold		
Harvey Jason	H	8. Ajay		Hold		
Peter Stormare	H	9. Dieter Stark		Hold		
Thomas Duffy	H	10. Dr. Burke		X	12:00 PM (test)	REPORT TO BACKLOT
Tommy Rosales	W	11. Carter		X	12:00 PM (test)	REPORT TO BACKLOT
Robert "Bobby Z" Zajonc	W	25. InGen Helicopter Pilot		X	7:00 PM	REPORT TO BACKLOT
Alan Purwin	SWF	25A. InGen Helicopter Pilot #2		5:00 PM	5:00 PM	REPORT TO RIVER ROAD LOT
Scott Shonka	W	32. InGen Worker		X	5:00 PM	REPORT TO RIVER ROAD LOT
Gary Hymes	W	X. Stunt Coordinator		X	5:00 PM	REPORT TO RIVER ROAD LOT
Jim Arnett	W	XX. Stunt Coordinator		X	6:00 PM	REPORT TO RIVER ROAD LOT
Pat Romano	W	XA. Utility Stunt		5:00 PM	6:00 PM	REPORT TO RIVER ROAD LOT
Kexi Johnston	W	XB. Utility Stunt		5:00 PM	6:00 PM	REPORT TO RIVER ROAD LOT
Cinda James (Sarah)	W	XC. Utility Stunt		5:00 PM	5:00 PM	REPORT TO RIVER ROAD LOT
Tom Morga (Ian)	W	XD. Utility Stunt		X		
David Rowden (Nick)	W	XE. Utility Stunt		Hold		
Lee Waddell (Eddie)	H	XF. Utility Stunt		Hold	5:00 PM	REPORT TO RIVER ROAD LOT
David Cadiente (Veterinarian)	H	XG. Utility Stunt		X	5:00 PM	REPORT TO RIVER ROAD LOT
Henry King	W	XH. Utility Stunt		X	5:00 PM	REPORT TO RIVER ROAD LOT
Chris Durand	W	XI. Utility Stunt		X	8:00 AM	REPORT TO RIVER ROAD LOT
Seth Arnett	W	XO. Utility Stunt		X	6:00 PM	REPORT TO RIVER ROAD LOT
Shawn Robinson	W	XP. Utility Stunt		5:00 PM	5:00 PM	REPORT TO RIVER ROAD LOT
Yuri Hinson	SWF	XQ. Utility Stunt		X	8:00 PM	REPORT TO RIVER ROAD LOT
Yun Hinson (Kelly)	W	XR. Utility Stunt		X	8:00 PM	REPORT TO RIVER ROAD LOT
Christopher Caso	W	RPTC. Puppeteer		X	8:00 PM	REPORT TO RIVER ROAD LOT
Chris Swift	W	RPTD. Puppeteer		X	8:00 PM	REPORT TO RIVER ROAD LOT
Rich Haugen	W	RPTE. Puppeteer		X	8:00 PM	REPORT TO RIVER ROAD LOT
Jeff Edwards	W	RPTF. Puppeteer		X	8:00 PM	REPORT TO RIVER ROAD LOT
Alan Scott	W	RPTG. Puppeteer				
Lynette Johnson	W	RPTH. Puppeteer				
Linday Macgowan	W	RPTI. Puppeteer				
David Covarrubias						

STAND-INS / PHOTO DOUBLES / ATMOSPHERE

STANDINS: 4 SI Utility (#1,2,3,5) @ 5:00 PM Report To River Road Parking Lot.

EXTRAS:

FITTINGS:

4 TOTAL STAND-INS
0 TOTAL PHOTO DOUBLES
0 TOTAL EXTRAS
0 TOTAL FITTINGS

NEAREST EMERGENCY HOSPITAL
Universal Hospital
7-2400

SPECIAL INSTRUCTIONS

COSTUMES: Sarah's bloody shirt.

ART DEPT./SET DRESSING: Rack of tools on wall.

SPECIAL EFFECTS: Mist, wet down, rain, avalanche of tiles, tiles sliding, rack of tools away and clank. Breakaway glass in jeep.

PROPS: Sarah's backpack, flashlight weapons, tiles.

SPECIAL EQUIPMENT: Titan Crane, Steadi Cam, 8-perf camera, Helicopter, camera Ship Helicopter.

VEHICLES: Abandoned car.

ELECTRIC: Searchlight effect, helicopter mounted searchlight, radio lights, 2 Musco lights, Nite Light.

SWS DINOSAURS: Raptors.

ILM: Poles and cutouts for reference. CGI shot on Raptor breaking thru glass.

AERIAL UNIT: Helicopter.

ADVANCE SCHEDULE

DATE	SC/SB	SCENE/STORYBOARD	SET/DESCRIPTION	PAGES	CAST	LOCATION
Mon	SC	153, 155, 155B	INT - KILN HOUSE - NIGHT	2 6/8	1,2,3,3X	Universal Studios Stage #22
	SB		Ian, Sarah, Kelly trapped inside. Raptor breaks in, chases them up the catwalks.		RPT	
Tues	SC	157	INT - SHED (FIXTURE) - NIGHT	1/8	2	Universal Studios Stage #12
11/4/96	SB	95-95B	Sarah hide in thru roof onto light fixture. It breaks.		2X	
thru			She crashes out the window.	2 2/8	6,7,8	
Wed.	SC		EXT - JUNGLE (BABY T - REX) - NIGHT		bRX	
11/6/96	SB		Roland has Baby T - Rex staked out. Ludlow (w/ guys), breaks as leg by accident.	1/8	7,8	
	SC	58 (pt. 1 of 2)	EXT - JUNGLE - HIGH HIDE (BABY T - REX) - NIGHT		bRX	
	SB	18, 18A-B	Baby T - Rex convulses. Roland and Ajay wait in a high hide.	2/8	7, 8 7X, 8X	
	SC		EXT - JUNGLE - HIGH HIDE (BABY T - REX) - NIGHT		bRX	
	SB	37A-B, 38, 39	Roland and Ajay see tranked in camp, prep crashing down. They climb down rope the high hide.	2/8	7,8 bRX	
	SC		EXT - JUNGLE (BABY T - REX) - NIGHT		bRX	
	SB	63	Male tranks Baby T -Rex, rescues s.			

UPM: D. Scott Easton **Key 2nd AD:** Sean Hoben, pager
1st AD: Sergio Mimica **2nd 2nd AD:** Lars Winther, pager

Printed: 11/1/96 8:30 AM

L.A. Production office phone:
100 Universal City Plaza, Trailer MT-11: Universal City, CA 91608

CREW LIST (continued)

TIME: 5:00 PM **DATE:** Friday, November 1, 1996

#	ITEM	CALL	NAME
1	COSTUME SUPERVISOR	O/C	SUE MOORE
1	SET COSTUMER		
1	SET COSTUMER	4:42 PM	KELLY PORTER
1	COSTUMER	4:42 PM	DALLAS DORNAN
1	COSTUMER	4:42 PM	MARIE KADERBECK
1	COSTUMER	per dept	BEAU DESMOND
1	KEY MAKE-UP ARTIST	per dept	PHYLLIS THURBER-MOFFIT
1	MAKE-UP ARTIST	4:30 PM	CHRISTINA SMITH
1	ADDL. MAKE-UP ARTIST	4:30 PM	CYNTHIA BARR-BRIGHT
1	ADDL. MAKE-UP ARTIST	4:30 PM	JOHN JACKSON
1	KEY HAIRSTYLIST		
1	HAIRSTYLIST	4:30 PM	JUDY CORY
1	ADDL. HAIRSTYLIST	4:30 PM	SUSAN SCHULER
1	CREATURE EFFECTS	W/N	KARYN HUSTON
1	SWS FX SUPERVISOR	O/C	STAN WINSTON
1	SWS FX SUPERVISOR		JOHN ROSENGRANT
1	SWS FX SUPERVISOR	8:00 PM	ALAN SCOTT
1	SWS FX SUPERVISOR	8:00 PM	SHANE MAHAN
1	EFFECTS TECHNICIAN		MARK "CRASH" McCREERY
1	EFFECTS TECHNICIAN		
1	EFFECTS TECHNICIAN	8:00 PM	LLOYD BALL
		8:00 PM	GLEN DERY
1	PUBLICIST		
1	STILL PHOTOGRAPHER	O/C	DON LEVY
1	MARKETING	5:00 PM	DAVID JAMES
1	PRODUCTION SUPERVISOR	O/C	JERRY SCHMITZ
1	LOCATION MANAGER	O/C	PETER TOBYANSEN
1	ASST. LOCATION MANAGER	O/C	MICHAEL HARO
X	SECURITY	O/C	ALEX REID
	POLICE	O/C	PER LOCATION
	FIRE		PER LOCATION
	CASTING DIRECTOR		PER LOCATION
	EXTRAS CASTING	O/C	JANET HIRSHENSON
	MEDIC	O/C	CENTRAL CASTING - TONY HOBBS
	MEDIC - CONSTRUCTION	5:00 PM	TODD ADELMAN
	UNIT PRODUCTION MANAGER	O/C	JUDY MALINOSKI
	PRODUCTION COORDINATOR	O/C	D. SCOTT EASTON
	ASST. PRODUCTION COORD.	O/C	SHERRY MARSHALL
	PRODUCTION SECRETARY	O/C	TODD LACHNIET
	OFFICE P.A.	O/C	STACIE SPEAKER
	OFFICE P.A.	O/C	STEVE PETYERAK
	ASSOCIATE PRODUCER	O/C	SCOTT OBERHOLTZER
	ASST. TO DIRECTOR	O/C	BONNIE CURTIS
	DIRECTOR'S P.A.	O/C	CRIS CLARKE
	ASST. TO PRODUCER	O/C	MARC FUSCO
	ASST. TO PRODUCER	O/C	ELYSE KLAITS
	ASST. TO PRODUCER	O/C	JENNIE DIETCH
	ASST. PRODUCER	O/C	DIANA TINKLEY
	ASST. PRODUCER	O/C	LESLIE BARNETT
	WRITER	O/C	MARK RUSSELL
	PRODUCTION ACCOUNTANT	O/C	JANICE NAEHU
	ACCOUNTANT	O/C	STEVIE LAZO
	ACCOUNTANT	O/C	KELLY RICHARDS RALSTON
	ACCOUNTANT	O/C	JAMES T. LINVILLE
	ACCOUNTANT	O/C	SHAUN McGOVERN
	CLERK	O/C	JOSH O'MALLEY
	ASST. ACCOUNTANT	O/C	NANCY HONEYCUTT
	ACCOUNTANT	O/C	KAY JORDAN
		O/C	EDWARD POVEDA
	EDITOR	O/C	MICHAEL KAHN
	EDITOR	O/C	PATRICK CRANE
		O/C	KEN BLACKWELL
		O/C	STEVE BAUERFEIN
		O/C	MICHAEL ALTMAN
		rdy @ 4:30 PM	TIM GONZALES
		rdy @ 4:30 PM	SERGIO TORAL
			GERARD ARNOULT
			Andrew Shourd, Jeff White, Daniels
		rdy @ 4:30 PM	
		rdy @ 11:00 PM	ready for drivers @ 10:30 PM
		O/C	DENNY CAIRA
		O/C	STEPHEN LUCE
		O/C	WAYNE WILLIAMS
		O/C	TRISH BARNHART
		per dept	SEE BELOW
		per dept	STEVE SORKIN
		per dept	STUMPY STINTON
		per dept	TERRY CRNIC
		per dept	BILL BALLARD
		per dept	GARY KINCADE
		per dept	LEO BAKER
		per dept	TAD VENGER
		per dept	JOHN MORELLO
		per dept	WALLY FRICK
		per dept	SERGIO OROSCO
		per dept	BOB CAWLEY JR
		per dept	GREG LANDIS
		per dept	BOB NEAL
		per dept	TBD
		per dept	TBD
		per dept	KELLY JORDAN
		per dept	GEORGE POWERS
		per dept	TBD
		per dept	TBD
		per dept	TINO CAIRA
		per dept	JEFF GOLD
		per dept	TBD
		per dept	BOB FISH
		per dept	FRED MOSHER
		per dept	FRED MOSHER
		per dept	ROBBIE STINTON
		per dept	TBD
		per dept	TBD
		per dept	TBD
		per dept	PEDRO ALEMAN
		per dept	MIKE SHANNON
		per dept	IER DEPT
			DENNIS CLARK
			DENNIS MARCHANT

Call to Wrap

5:00 P.M.

It is just cool enough to portend a cold night, but no one is complaining. The previous night, at this same location, temperatures dipped to the high thirties, a bitter cold by Los Angeles standards. Tonight, although nippy, promises to be better. Even so, makeup supervisor Christina Smith is taking no chances. She has been given the nickname "Queen of Warm" by the crew for reasons that become obvious as soon as she wanders by, covered from head to toe in scarves, socks, gloves, sweatshirt, sweatpants, and hooded parka.

The emotional climate on the set is as temperate as the weather. Crew members, with ever-present radios on their heads, engage in their respective tasks at a brisk pace, preparing for the six o'clock shooting call—but there is no panic in the air. The schedule's halfway mark has been passed and, up to now, the shoot has gone remarkably well.

The winding road leading to this uppermost region of the backlot is most frequently traveled by trams for the Universal Studios Hollywood Tour, which typically turn back at the house in which "Mother" tormented motel proprietor Norman Bates in Alfred Hitchcock's *Psycho.* As a result, tourists usually do not see what lies beyond the house—a pond and a large, empty expanse of land, rising at the far end to a height of maybe a hundred feet, forming a cliff of soil, small trees, and brush.

Tonight, however, the field reveals an arena in which mankind and nature appear to have duked it out—and nature won. Settled within a gloriously green and rich landscape is a cluster of decaying buildings, covered in vines and moss, like week-old Chia pets. Pipes that must have served some purpose at some time are cracked and rusted, as are the vehicles with flattened tires scattered willy-nilly throughout the complex. A hurricane swept through this place, and it shows.

The setting is the InGen laboratory compound at Site B—the place in which, almost ten years ago, InGen scientists performed feats of genetic engineering that

Opposite: The call sheet for November 1, 1996. *Below:* The laboratory compound set on the Universal backlot.

Above: The set was dressed with debris and rusted vehicles to suggest the long-abandoned state of the compound. *Top, right, and far right:* Crew member Drew Petrotta and prop master Jerry Moss prepare for the night's shoot.

ultimately led to the cloning of dinosaurs for John Hammond's Jurassic Park. A multistory lab building at one end is the compound's most imposing structure. A smattering of smaller buildings are laid out below. A tall, rustic-looking gate at the far end serves as the main entrance; and beyond the gate lies the source of the compound's power supply, the geothermal plant.

Every building, every vehicle, every rusted pipe, and, in fact, every tree is part of the set created for the filming of the raptor chase sequence in *The Lost World*. Director of photography Janusz Kaminski has artfully illuminated the area to retain the quality of moonlight. Dolly track has been laid, atop of which sit tall camera cranes. A water truck that will moisten the area immediately prior to each take stands by. Monitors and sound equipment are set up. In a humorous nod to the nearness of the *Psycho* house, a makeshift sign with the caricatured image of Alfred Hitchcock and the words "Alfred is watching" is tacked onto an equipment cart.

5:15 P.M.

Jeff Goldblum, Julianne Moore, Vince Vaughn, and Vanessa Lee Chester have arrived for their five o'clock makeup and wardrobe call. Makeup includes not only the standard application required to ensure the actors' faces read under the bright film lights, but also a good "muddying-up" to suggest the rugged conditions the characters have endured during their brief but terrifying sojourn in the lost world of Isla Sorna. The gooey simulated mud is planted on their clothing as well, after the actors have finished in makeup and donned their costumes.

5:45 P.M.

Producer Jerry Molen has arrived on the set, after an afternoon of scouting locations in Newhall, about fifty miles north of Los Angeles. Molen is aware of everything that is scheduled to happen this evening, and he is here—along with Colin Wilson—to make sure that it does. "When we wrapped last night," Molen explains, "Steven gave us a setup for what he wanted to do tonight; and that information was then distributed to the various crews. Usually, we can tell from the setup how long it will take for the crews to get everything ready. Consequently, we can give Steven a time to show up, and we'll be ready by the time he gets here."

As the six o'clock shooting time approaches, Molen and Wilson act as troubleshooters, dealing with the inevitable problems and questions that arise on the set. The most pressing concern is the scheduling of aerial photography slated for later in the evening. Spielberg's intention is to capture footage of the rescue helicopter's approach to the

lab rooftop, and its subsequent takeoff—a logistically complicated series of shots that may cut in too much on the available time for the raptor chase. "There are some concerns and questions as to whether or not we can finish all of those helicopter shots tonight," Molen says. "So, right now, we're trying to get some answers to that very big question."

6:18 P.M.

Six o'clock has come and gone, and although no cameras have rolled, the set is abuzz with activity. Michael Lantieri confers with effects foreman Don Elliott and other members of his on-set effects crew. Shots in the raptor chase—scheduled for the second half of the night—will demand most of the effects crew's attention tonight. Breakaway glass windows have been installed in buildings and vehicles to accommodate raptor break-ins. To provide interaction and suggest the impact of computer generated raptors, the side of a vehicle has been equipped with pneumatics to make it buckle on cue, and the metal wall of a building has been rigged to tear itself wide open.

Above: Jeff Goldblum's first stop is the makeup trailer, where Christina Smith readies the actor for filming. *Below, left:* Crew members prepare sheets of breakaway glass that will be used for shots of raptors breaking into buildings and cars during the compound chase scene.

6:35 P.M.

The water truck noisily sprays down the entire set, making it even more muddy than it was when the crew arrived. The wet-down not only adds a humid, jungly atmosphere to the set, it serves continuity purposes, since rain has already been established during the previous two nights of filming—some of it courtesy of Mother Nature.

In preparation for the first shot of the evening, the crew has focused its attention on the dinosaur bone yard laid out at

Early in the evening, the crew prepares for a long, tracking shot of the discovery of the lab compound. As laid out, the set featured a dinosaur boneyard leading into a geothermal plant and the compound's main gates.

the far end of the set. Janusz Kaminski directs the lighting of the area from atop a Chapman Titan crane, twenty-five feet in the air. A stand-in for Vince Vaughn takes his position in the bone yard so that Kaminski and the camera crew can make adjustments before the actor steps into the shot.

6:55 P.M.

The four principal actors have been called to the set. Goldblum's face is moistened to simulate perspiration, and Julianne Moore is rubbed down with fake mud by the makeup and wardrobe teams. Reference photos from the night before—

simple Polaroids—are held up to the actors to check continuity. A last minute check of the surroundings is also being attended to by the greens crew, which has dressed the set with hundreds of potted plants and trees to match the thick vegetation of the Northern California locations. Satisfied that everything is in place, greensman Kevin Mangan exits the shooting area and stands at the sidelines, casually pulling toothpick-size splinters out of the palm of his hand. "I don't like to wear gloves," he says with a nonchalant shrug.

7:20 P.M.

Spielberg arrives, looking fresh and energetic, despite the fact that he has spent all day cutting the film with editor Michael Kahn. Spielberg's presence on the set signals the start of the night's shoot; within five minutes everyone is ready for a rehearsal of the first shot. "Quiet please" is heard and instantly acknowledged by the hundred-some crew people lined up out of camera range. At Spielberg's command, Vince Vaughn begins to run through a giant skeletal rib cage, followed by Steadicam operator Chris Haarhoff. Strapped onto a harness worn by the operator and attached to a counterweighted rig, the Steadicam allows

Haarhoff to run behind the actor, while maintaining a smooth, even quality in the handheld shot.

After two more rehearsals of the scene—which ends with Vaughn emerging from the bone yard and discovering the laboratory compound—Spielberg is ready to roll film. Immediately prior to shooting, fog machines hidden within the foliage expel a bluish-white mist; a handheld version is used to fog up the immediate shooting area; a crew member goes in to rake out shoe prints from the soil; and the water truck is signaled to spray down the set.

Spielberg, Kaminski, and Kathy Kennedy are seated behind a camera monitor; and when all is ready, Spielberg jumps up from his director's chair and

Top, left: Dramatic atmosphere was provided by automatic and hand-held fog machines. *Top, right:* After tumbling down a hill, the characters find themselves in the dinosaur boneyard.

Top, left: Steven Spielberg and Kathy Kennedy on the compound set. *Right:* Several hours were devoted to the filming of the rescue helicopter's approach and lab rooftop landing. *Above, left:* Vanessa Lee Chester and Vince Vaughn play checkers between setups.

shouts, "Okay guys! Picture's up!" "Rolling!" is heard from the assistant directors, and at the sound of Spielberg's "Action," Vaughn goes through the now familiar routine inside the giant rib cage.

Take 1 is followed by a brief conference between director and actor. "Vince, when you come out, you've got to look around you and appreciate the wonder of all this," Spielberg says, waving his hand to indicate the magnificent compound nestled within the jungle. Vaughn nods in understanding and returns to his place on the set. Several more takes are required; but at Take 7, Spielberg smiles and says, "Very nice."

It is 8:26, and the first shot of the night is in the can.

9:00 P.M.

The compound reveal, Nick's run through the rib cage, and shots of Malcolm, Sarah, and Kelly following have all been committed to film. The crew now begins to set up for shots of the helicopter landing on the lab roof. The actors will not be needed for a while, and so they scatter—Julianne Moore and Jeff Goldblum to their respective trailers; Vince Vaughn and Vanessa Lee Chester to the craft services table, where they grab snacks and then settle onto chairs to play checkers or handheld video games.

Other waiting company members are the ten creature effects technicians from the Stan Winston Studio. Supervisors

Shane Mahan and Alan Scott and their crew arrived on the set at eight o'clock and immediately checked in with producers Jerry Molen and Colin Wilson to establish the game plan for the night. "They had all the information in terms of what Steven wanted to do tonight," Mahan explains, "and they let us know approximately what time we'd be working. Then I filled in the rest of our crew. We dished out radios and prepped everything so we'd be ready. Once they tell us it's time to go, we'll just run in and do it."

Visual effects supervisor Dennis Muren, animation director Randy Dutra, and match-move technician Jack Haye are also awaiting their next up. It's their second night on the laboratory compound set, and tonight they're slated to shoot plates for the CG raptor chase. Haye will use a laser surveying system to take exact measurements for each CG setup. "When we get to doing our CG shots later on," Muren explains, "that information will cut in half, or more, the amount of time it will take to put our computer model into the scene."

After shooting two plates at the beginning of their evening, the ILM crew members are now in waiting mode as take after take is filmed of the helicopter landing and lifting off. When the helicopter footage is captured, the ILM crew will set up for the filming of a raptor chasing Malcolm into a car, then breaking the glass and crashing into the vehicle interior—a continuation of the scene the crew was working on the previous night. "We have to get it tonight," Muren notes, "and we *will* get it tonight, because Steven is very good about sticking to the schedule. He juggles things, does little on-the-spot rewrites—anything he has to do to make the schedule."

9:50 P.M.

Logistical details have been worked out between the helicopter pilot and the grounded film crew. Now, the four principal actors are called back to the set for a

The rescue helicopter was piloted by veteran film pilot "Bobby Z" Zajonc.

```
149  CONTINUED:  2                                      149

                        KELLY
               WHAT ARE YOU GOING TO DO?!

                       MALCOLM
            I LOVE YOU!  RUN LIKE HELL!

     He shoves her, hard, and she takes off running, toward the
     building Sarah went in.  The raptor lunges in that direction,
     to pursue her, but Malcolm cuts it off, SHOUTING as he does
     so.

     The raptor stops, surprised.  Malcolm SCREAMS at it.  The
     raptor cocks its head curiously.  Lotta fight in this animal.

     Malcolm charges straight at the raptor, SCREAMING, pounding
     his chest.  For about three seconds, he looks great --

     -- but the raptor doesn't run.  Instead, it opens its mouth
     wide and SNARLS right back.

     Malcolm skids to a halt.  That was pretty much it for his
     attack plan.  He looks behind him, just in time to see Kelly
     make it into the metal building.  But that's much too far for
     him now.  He darts between the idled gasoline pumps and into
     the gas station building, closing the door behind him.

     The raptor bounds after him, SLAMMING into the door.

     Meeting resistance, it bounces off, notices the plate glass
     window next to the door, and pounces at that.  The window
     SHATTERS and the raptor clings to the ledge, staring inside,
     its tail hanging out.

     Just as it gets inside, Malcolm opens the door and comes back
     out, keeping the piece of wall between them.  The raptor
     whirls and springs, forcing him back inside, through the door
     again.

     Willing to play along, the raptor turns and jumps through the
     window again.
```

shot of the characters making a desperate, final run all the way from the base of the lab building to the rooftop pad where the helicopter is waiting. Designed as a long, continuous shot, this last dash is filmed by Steadicam operator Chris Haarhoff, who runs on the heels of the actors as take after take is executed. The repeated takes of running full-speed up the lab stairway requires a high level of fitness, especially from Haarhoff who is loaded down with the camera and harness. All appear equal to the task. Exhausted but smiling, Julianne Moore leaves the set once a satisfactory take is captured. "That was exhilarating," Moore says between breaths. "I *loved* doing that shot!"

Landings and lift-offs continue for nearly two hours, filling the backlot area with the deafening roar of helicopter blades. Such shots are notoriously difficult because they involve the radio coordination of the ground-based film crew and the aerial pilots—in this case, Robert "Bobby Z" Zajonc. After one take, lights are adjusted to more properly illuminate the approaching chopper in the night sky.

Another take is ruined by a slight focus inaccuracy. Another is unacceptable due to the helicopter's incorrect positioning. It is well after eleven o'clock when the helicopter departs for the last time and quiet is restored on the set.

11:45 P.M.

Vanessa Lee Chester's legally mandated twelve-thirty A.M. wrap time is approaching, and Spielberg has one more shot he must get with the young actress—Kelly and Sarah running for shelter inside the three-story kiln building. The tracking shot—which starts at the Jeep where Malcolm is warding off raptors—will follow Julianne Moore and Chester as they run across a distance of several yards to the kiln, enter the building and slam the door. In the final movie, a CG raptor will be right at their heels.

The Winston crew sets up the full-body raptor at the Jeep, where it will be puppeteered to snarl and snap at the three characters. Even at rest, it looks menac-ing. The actors have taken their places next to the Jeep, and they watch as the puppeteers—stationed out of camera range, thirty feet away—put the raptor through some practice paces.

"We gotta go *now*," Spielberg announces at 12:05. In twenty-five more minutes, Vanessa will be gone. A quick rehearsal is conducted. Moore's brilliant red, braided hair is attended to. Kaminski makes a last minute lighting adjustment. Painfully aware of the time restrictions, Spielberg calls for the cameras to roll and then shoots three takes in rapid succession. Jeff Goldblum darts around the Jeep, trying to keep the vehicle between himself and the raptor, shouting at Kelly and Sarah to run. Moore and Chester make their desperate dash toward the kiln, the camera panning with them. Stan Winston stands immediately to the director's right, quietly whispering performance directions to his crew through his radio headset. "Go again," Spielberg says after the first take, noting that the hydraulic raptor did "something weird" with its camera-side forearm. Less than a minute later they do it again; and then one more time, now with the camera a bit closer to the running actors.

Before a fourth take is attempted, crew members hurriedly bury a lighting cable lying on the ground near the Jeep. Precious time is still ticking, and Spielberg is a little impatient when he asks, "Why are you doing that? This is a 50mm lens—we won't see that cable."

"Because Vanessa and Julianne are tripping over it," an A.D. answers.

"Good reason," Spielberg says, turning back to his monitor.

Two more takes and Spielberg has not yet seen his shot. It is 12:19, and he has Vanessa for only eleven minutes more. At

Opposite page, top left: The crew sets up for a shot of Sarah, Kelly, and Ian during the raptor chase. To suggest the CG raptor's impact, Moore was harnessed and yanked to the ground. *Top, right:* Since many of the night's shots would feature CG raptors, Goldblum and the other actors spent a good part of the night dodging invisible predators. *Middle, right:* A mechanical raptor was employed for a shot of Ian distracting the animal as Sarah and Kelly run for the shelter of the kiln. *This page, left:* Creature effects supervisor Shane Mahan stands by with a mechanical raptor rig. *Above:* Goldblum confers with Spielberg prior to filming another raptor chase shot.

Take 6, the raptor's forearm is again moving a bit stiffly. On his radio, Winston immediately relays the message to his crew, instructing them to find out what's wrong. Within seconds Shane Mahan reports that a cable connection near the raptor appears to have come loose. It is a simple matter to fix, but there is no time. Spielberg simply instructs the cameraman to reframe the shot slightly so the offending appendage will be excluded. Three more takes are shot, each requiring a slight adjustment of the camera or the actors' performances.

Take 9 is the one; and Spielberg says, "Print." It is 12:27. Spielberg puts his remaining three minutes to good use, quickly shooting a reaction close-up of Vanessa.

At twelve-thirty sharp, Spielberg and the entire crew warmly bid Vanessa goodnight.

12:37 A.M.

After filming a few reaction shots of Goldblum and Moore, lunch is called. It hardly seems the appropriate term for the middle-of-the-night meal, but "lunch" always refers to the hour-long, mid-shooting-day break, regardless of the time of day that halfway mark is met.

The crew gratefully heads for the catering tent set up at the edge of the adjacent field. Mealtimes are typically lighthearted and boisterous, but this one is especially so: Tonight is Friday, the end of a long week of night shooting. It is also visual effects supervisor Dennis Muren's fiftieth birthday, and a large decorated cake is delivered to him, along with a rousing rendition of "Happy Birthday." The celebration appears to be a real surprise to the quiet, unassuming Muren; and the crew's delight in honoring him is just as evident. After a twenty-some-year career, Dennis Muren is one of the most loved and respected craftsmen in the film industry.

There are no speeches. Muren merely says a quiet "thank you" and smiles.

2:03 A.M.

Back from lunch, Julianne Moore and Jeff Goldblum are being led through the choreography for a scene around an upturned vehicle. Both actors listen intently to what Spielberg has to say, then rehearse their actions several times as the camera and lights are set up. "What I like most about Steven," Moore says, "is how clear he is about what he needs in a scene. He's also very blunt. After a take, he has said things like, 'I didn't believe you were scared by that raptor just now—and if you aren't scared, the audience won't be scared.' I love that. It is refreshingly straightforward, and I think it makes him a terrific director for actors.

"I also appreciate how quickly he works. I don't like to do twenty takes in a scene. Either I'm going to get it in the beginning or I'm not going to get it—so it isn't worthwhile to me to do it over and over again. With this movie, there are all of these other elements to be pulled in,

The 1 A.M. "lunch." Dennis Muren is center.

along with the performances, and Steven still manages to get the shots quickly. A lot of that has to do with his preparedness, the crew's preparedness. They all come together, and Steven gets the shot—just like that."

2:24 A.M.

The crew is preparing for a scene in and around the small gas station building,

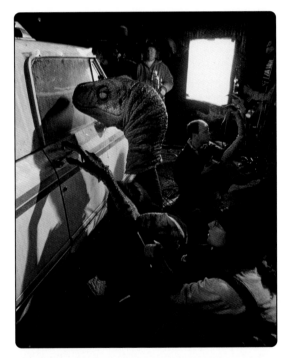

where Malcolm has entered at some point in the chase. In this particular scene, a raptor will leap through the large glass window, and Malcolm will run out, darting into the front seat of an abandoned truck nearby. The raptor follows, eventually breaking the glass of the truck window and entering the vehicle.

As the crew sets up, Goldblum finds a quiet, dark corner of the set where he goes through his actions over and over again. "We've had very little rehearsal time on this movie," he explains. "When we get to the set, we are going into these scenes cold. So I work things out and rehearse, either by myself or with Steven." These self-styled rehearsals are even more critical when, like tonight, a CG character is involved in a scene. "Sometimes I rehearse a little bit with the CGI people, so they can tell me exactly where the dinosaurs are going to be, and I can figure out where and how I need to react to them. I will say to Dennis Muren, 'Hey—you be the raptor and show me what it is going to be doing.'"

Below, middle: Stan Winston in radio communication with his puppeteering crew. *Below, left, and bottom, left:* An insert raptor head is positioned for a shot of the predator breaking a vehicle window. The insert head was built of stronger materials to withstand repeated impact. *Bottom, right:* A separate tail, manipulated from below, created the illusion of a head-to-toe animal from the perspective of the car interior.

Ian recoils as the raptor breaks into the vehicle.

2:37 A.M.

The company moves on to shots around and in the truck. Dolly track is laid down to accommodate the camera, which will be tracking Malcolm's approach. The Winston crew rehearses with the insert raptor head that will peer into the truck, then break the window. "We are using the insert head so that it can actually smash through breakaway glass and other materials," Shane Mahan explains. "We can't risk doing those kinds of actions with the hydraulic version,

because it has mechanisms that are very delicate and they would be damaged by that kind of abuse. The insert head is much tougher."

Although the short scene at the truck window will be initiated with the mechanical head, following cuts will feature the CG version. For that reason, special effects foreman Don Elliott and his crew are crouched at the truck's wheel base to rehearse the timing of their next gag—the simple rocking of the truck to suggest the raptor's assault on the vehicle.

All is ready when Spielberg suddenly has an idea. "Can we get CO_2 on the window when the raptor appears, like we had in the last movie?" He's referring to the shot of the raptor at the kitchen door in *Jurassic Park*, when a glass pane is fogged up by the snorting animal. Elliott complies.

4:00 A.M.

Everyone is getting tired. The graveyard shift is notoriously hard on the human body, and it shows on the faces of the crew members as they continue to shoot footage of Malcolm and the raptor at the truck. The last shot was captured half an hour ago, and now they're working on an interior POV as the raptor peers

Final ILM composite shows the raptors at the kiln as Ian watches.

into the truck window. They're on Take 6 when Spielberg revises the camera movement slightly. "Give me a slow push-in this time," Spielberg says. "You know, so it looks like *NYPD Blue*." The cameraman seems to understand the reference, and Take 7 is a good one.

As they set up for the raptor's POV, which will reveal Malcolm inside the vehicle, the lights are dimmed on the set to adjust for the early morning sky, which is getting noticeably lighter with the passing of each minute. In another hour or so it will be too light to continue shooting the night scene—but there are still five shots to go, and Spielberg intends to get them. He works even more quickly now, calling for take after take, with the camera rolling continuously.

4:38 A.M.

The fatigue is palpable. A good third of the crew can be seen yawning. People lean against whatever they can find. A movie set offers few places to sit down—a clear indication of how little sitting is involved in the making of movies. One who isn't yawning is Stan Winston, a man of extraordinarily high energy. Finding himself between setups, Winston tap dances to stay warm.

4:45 A.M.

The mechanical raptors are done for the night, and the Winston crew begins the nearly two-hour process of loading everything onto a truck. It is a heavy-duty, machinery-aided process since each raptor rig weighs approximately 350 pounds.

Final setup is called. The craft services table is broken down. The shooting day is almost over.

But Spielberg presses on. Another POV from inside the truck is shot. Additional panes of breakaway glass are installed.

Overhead, the sky is turning blue.

5:31 A.M.

There is one last setup on the night's schedule, a Steadicam shot of Malcolm running from the truck to the kiln building. It is the same building Julianne Moore and Vanessa Lee Chester were filmed entering five hours ago. With day breaking, there is no time for rehearsal, no time for multiple takes, no time for errors. "Shoot against the light," Spielberg instructs the Steadicam operator; then, to no one in particular, "We've got to get this, man." And he does.

It is 5:47, and the day's shoot for *The Lost World* has wrapped.

CHAPTER 11

AN INTERVIEW
WITH

Steven Spielberg

Why did you choose The Lost World *as your first project after a three-year hiatus from directing?*

I guess I realized that what I really wanted to do was direct. I had started a company and done a lot of other things in those three years, but somehow, directing movies got lost in the mix. So I was ready to return to it, and I had always wanted to do a sequel to *Jurassic Park*—both because of the popular demand and because I'd had such a great time making the first film. I wanted to revisit the past a little bit.

The sequel would be based on Michael Crichton's novel. What were your immediate impressions of the book?

Well, when I first heard that Michael was going to write the book and that he was thinking of calling it *The Lost World*, I was thrilled because I'm a big fan of Sir Arthur Conan Doyle's book *The Lost World*. I was compelled by the idea of being inside a prehistoric world that exists today—not behind electrified fences, not in a theme park, but in a world without the intervention of man. I thought, "Wow, what a great story."

Jurassic Park *ushered in new technologies for filmmaking, particularly in regard to computer graphics. How did you intend to reach beyond that groundbreaking film with* The Lost World?

Mainly by making sure that *The Lost World* was a really good story. It was the story that justified doing a sequel,

not the technology. CGI has improved since the first movie, and the artistry of the people involved has also improved. So there was a good chance that the dinosaurs would look even more believable than they had in the last adventure. But it was really the story that compelled me to make this movie. If I hadn't found a story I was interested in, *Jurassic Park* would have remained just a nice memory for me.

You actually began storyboarding The Lost World *nearly two years before the movie was released, and a year before you started shooting. Why did you get involved in storyboarding so early?*

A movie like this needs at least a year to eighteen months of prep time, because it takes so long just to build the animals. To prepare a production of this size, you can't just throw it together in the normal four-month prep you might have for a

drama or comedy. You need months and months, even years.

The story of The Lost World *centers on two groups of people—the hunters and the gatherers—each with its own mission and philosophy. How do the differences in those two groups generate the story's dramatic tension?*

Drama is rubbing two sticks together and seeing what is set aflame. In this story, what we're bringing together are these hunters and this group of dinosaur advocates. The second group isn't so far out there that they make you reel from the political correctness of it all; but they are, in fact, as aggressive in trying to protect this environment as the hunters are in trying to exploit it. So these two groups come together and end up having to band together just to survive. And that creates more than just a lot of running from dinosaurs—there's a lot of good emotional human drama, as well.

How has the Ian Malcolm character changed from the first movie to this one?

I think Ian in this film is much more of a constructive force in moving the adventure forward. In the first film, Malcolm was the critic. He sat around badmouthing everybody and telling them where they were wrong; and as it turned out, he was right. But in *The Lost World,* he is, in a sense, leading the journey, rather than just being along for the ride.

One of the new characters in the movie is Sarah Harding, the paleontologist and Malcolm's love interest. Would you talk about her character, and your choice of Julianne Moore for the role?

Julianne is a wonderful actress, and I'd wanted to work with her for years. I even twisted the part of Sarah around to fit Julianne—although, she is such a good actress, she could have done the part whether it was designed for her or not. Sarah is studying nurturing behavior among carnivores, so she is opening up a new field of study. And she uses this opportunity to explore her beliefs, as any paleontologist would. She has an insatiable curiosity.

One of the most interesting characters is Roland, the hunter who is looking to go up against the T-rex, the ultimate predator. What was it about Pete Postlethwaite that made you think of him for the role?

When I saw him in *In the Name of the Father* I thought, "There's an actor I would love to work with someday." I was a big, big fan of his. I always imagined working with Pete in a kind of intellectual world, with him in the part of a priest or a father, probably because my mind had been skewed by his performance in that movie—and it came to me that he would be great for Roland.

What went into your decision to cast Peter Stormare as Dieter?

I saw him in *Fargo* and I wondered who this scary guy with the whitish hair was. David Koepp had already written the character of Dieter; and, in my mind, Peter Stormare began to fit David's profile of who this guy should be. So I arranged to meet with Peter, and I was actually intimidated because I was expecting to meet this coldhearted maniac from *Fargo*. But then I walked into the office and here was this sweet, gentle man who was noth-

ing at all like the character he'd played. He was the polar opposite of the guy he played in *Fargo*; and I thought, well, this guy can act anything—I gotta have him in my movie. I offered him the part five minutes later.

Vince Vaughn is a new face—how did you find him and what did you see in him?

I was basically looking for a new movie star to play Nick Van Owen—a new mid-twenties American icon. That's hard to find. You only find those once every six or seven years. Tom Cruise came along, and then a few years later George Clooney came along; and a few years after that, Matthew McConaughey came along. I was looking for somebody with that kind of charisma. And then I saw *Swingers*, a very low-budget picture, and I thought Vince was great in it, and very funny. And when I met him, I saw somebody who wasn't what he purported to be

in that role. I always admire actors who aren't themselves in the movies they make. I thought Vince was a character actor as well as a leading man, and that he would be great in the cast. So I invited him to join.

One of the most thrilling sequences in this movie is the one in which the T-rexes attack the trailer at the cliff. Dramatically, what were you aiming for with that scene?

Pure pleasure and adventure—something that would make the audience shriek and cover their eyes. I always keep the audience in mind on a movie like this. The audience comes first, even before me. I may have my own secret desires, and I might make another kind of movie to express those, but I really think of the audience when I am making a *Jurassic Park* or a *Lost World*.

Since the technology has improved so much, were you interested in employing CG

much more freely in The Lost World, *with many more CG shots than what had been in the first movie?*

Not really, because they're still expensive. I felt I had to be frugal and restrain my imagination a little bit, to keep the film from becoming too costly. I didn't want to make a sequel that undergrossed and overcost the original. I tried very hard to keep the CGI shots down, and we wound up with about thirty more than we had in the first film.

Like the first movie, there are not only computer generated dinosaurs in The Lost World, *but also a variety of animatronic dinosaurs, designed and executed by Stan Winston. Did you raise the stakes in terms of what you wanted to accomplish with the animatronic characters?*

Stan himself raised the stakes. He wanted to retool all of the animals and give them even more smooth, lifelike movements. I thought he did an amazing job on the first movie; but Stan is an artist, and so he's never satisfied with his work. He always wants to improve it— and he really did for this show. The mechanical dinosaurs are indistinguishable from the CGI animals.

Jurassic Park's *trump card was that it had 3-D animated dinosaurs—something the audience had never seen before. What do you think audiences will get from* The Lost World, *since they'll know walking in that they're going to see 3-D dinosaurs?*

Well, the audience knew walking into *Jurassic Park* that they were going to see dinosaurs—they were just amazed that the dinosaurs looked as real as they did. I

think everybody—myself included—was expecting some variation of Ray Harryhausen's brilliant stop-motion photography. But CGI gave us a new yardstick to measure against the real world, and people were startled by that, and a little awestruck. In this movie, we don't have the element of surprise. People will come in expecting the same level of technology and the same level of reality in the animals. But our response to that expectation was to make a different, more dramatic movie, while keeping the humor and suspense and all of the things that audiences had liked about the first movie. I think that's what people want in a sequel, anyway. They want to roll up their sleeves and fall right back into that adventure.

Only eight weeks after wrapping prinicipal photography on The Lost World, *Steven Spielberg left for the East Coast to begin filming* Amistad, *his next movie.*

Film Credits

PRODUCTION STAFF

Directed by....STEVEN SPIELBERG
Screenplay by....DAVID KOEPP
Based on the novel *The Lost World* by.....MICHAEL CRICHTON
Produced by....GERALD R. MOLEN and COLIN WILSON
Executive Producer....KATHLEEN KENNEDY
Director of Photography....JANUSZ KAMINSKI, A.S.C.
Production Designer....RICK CARTER
Film Editor....MICHAEL KAHN, A.C.E.
Music by....JOHN WILLIAMS
JEFF GOLDBLUM
JULIANNE MOORE
PETE POSTLETHWAITE
ARLISS HOWARD
RICHARD ATTENBOROUGH
VINCE VAUGHN
VANESSA LEE CHESTER
PETER STORMARE
HARVEY JASON
RICHARD SCHIFF
THOMAS F. DUFFY
JOSEPH MAZZELLO
ARIANA RICHARDS
Associate Producer....BONNIE CURTIS
Unit Production Manager....D. SCOTT EASTON
First Assistant Director....SERGIO MIMICA-GEZZAN
Second Assistant Director....SEAN HOBIN
Full Motion Dinosaurs by....DENNIS MUREN, A.S.C.
Live Action Dinosaurs by....STAN WINSTON
Special Dinosaur Effects by....MICHAEL LANTIERI
Casting by....JANET HIRSHENSON, C.S.A., and JANE JENKINS, C.S.A.
Dinosaur Supervisor....RANDAL M. DUTRA
Visual Effects Producer....NED GORMAN
Production Supervisor....PETER "TOBY" TOBYANSEN
2nd Unit Director....DAVID KOEPP
Sound Design....GARY RYDSTROM
Supervising Sound Editor....RICHARD HYMNS
Production Sound....RON JUDKINS, ROBERT JACKSON
Art Director....JIM TEEGARDEN
Costume Supervisor....SUE MOORE
Set Decorator....GARY PETTIS
Property Master....JERRY MOSS
Art Directors....LAUREN POLIZZI, PAUL SONSKI
Assistant Art Directors....DAVE LOWERY, JOHN BERGER, MATT CODD, SEAN HARGREAVES
Illustrators....STEFAN DECHANT, JAMES OXFORD, WARREN MANSER
Set Designers....PAMELA KLAMER, LINDA KING
"A" Camera Operator....MITCH DUBIN
Steadicam "B" Camera Operator....CHRIS HAARHOFF
"A" Camera Focus Puller....STEVEN MEIZLER
"A" Camera 2nd Assistant....MARK SPATH
"B" Camera Focus Puller/Steadicam Focus Puller....KARL OWENS
"B" Camera 2nd Assistant/Crane Technician....TOM JORDAN
Key Loader....TIM GAYLORD
Camera Assistant (PA)....DAVID O'BRIEN
Camera Intern....TOMOMI ITAYA
ILM Camera Assistant Vista Vision....MARK GUTTERUD
Stunt Coordinators....M. JAMES ARNETT, GARY HYMES
Assistant Stunt Coordinator....PAT ROMANO
Marine Coordinator....C. RANSOM WALROD
Still Photographer....DAVID JAMES
Video Engineer....DANIEL P. MOORE
Script Supervisor....ANA MARIA QUINTANA
Sound Utility....TOVE BLUE
Key Costumers....MARIE KADERBECK, MITCHELL KENNEY
Set Costumers....KELLY PORTER, MARCI JOHNSON, DALLAS DORNAN
Costumer....BEAU DESMOND
Textile Effects....PHYLLIS THURBER-MOFFIT
Staff Assistant....DANNY DIRKS
Assistant Property Master....DREW PETROTTA
Assistant Props....MAURA MOSS, MARK BROWN
2nd 2nd Assistant Director....LARS WINTHER
Additional 2nd Assistant Director/Eureka....AMY HUGHES
Dga Trainee....WILFREN J. KILLIAN
Unit Publicist....DON LEVY
Production Office Coordinator....SHERRY MARSHALL
Assistant Production Coordinator....TODD LACHNIET
Production Secretary....STACIE L. SPEAKER
Office Production Assistants....STEVE P. PETYERAK, SCOTT J. OBERHOLTZER, GARY L. STEIN, ANGELA TILLSON
Supervising Key Makeup Artist....CHRISTINA SMITH
Makeup Artists....CYNTHIA BARR-BRIGHT, MATTHEW MUNGLE
Body Makeup....GINA RYLANDER
Key Hairstylist....JUDY ALEXANDER-CORY
Hairstylists....SUSAN SCHULER, KARYN L. HUSTON
Gaffer....DAVID DEVLIN
Best Boy Electric....JAREK GORCZYCKI
Universal Best Boy....O'SHANA WALKER
Electricians....MAREK BOJSZA, LARRY RICHARDSON, PATRICK HOESCHEN, DANIEL WINDELS
Dimmer Board Operator....MICHAEL LAMBERT
Rigging Gaffer....BRIAN LUKAS
Best Boy Rigging Electric....PAUL AVERY
Rigging Electrics....ERIK BUTTERS, SCOTT "SCOOTER" MEDCALF, ROBERT S. DILLEY, JEFFREY RENILE, STEVE KAGEN, CHRIS ZAMOSCIANYK
Universal Electric....JOHN "T. J." TRUJILLO
Key Grip....JIM KWIATKOWSKI
Best Boy Grip....KEVIN ERB
Dolly Grip....JACK GLENN
Grips....JACOB CERRONE, KRASH KOWAL, DAN COSCIA, RALPH SCHERER, SCOTT FROSCHAUER, JAMES WALSH, BRENT JONES
Key Rigging Grip....CHARLEY H. GILLERAN
Best Boy Rigging Grip....ROBERT PRESTON
Rigging Grips....JERRY DAY, STEVE OWEN, KEVIN FAHEY, JAYNE ROY
Special Effects Foreman....DON ELLIOTT
Shop Foreman....TOM PAHK
Car Shop Foreman....THOMAS R. HOMSHER
Special Effects....RON CIESIELSKI, JOHN OSSELLO, CORY FAUCHER, ROBIN REILLY, LOUIE LANTIERI, BRIAN TIPTON, MATTHEW MCDONNELL, TOM TOKUNAGA, DAN OSSELLO
Visual Effects Liaison....MICHAEL FALLAVOLLITA
Conceptual Artist....JOHN BELL
Model Makers....GREG ARONOWITZ, EDITH GONZALES, ROBERT SHERWOOD
Art Department Coordinator....KACY MAGEDMAN
Assistant Art Department Coordinator....MARK A. KURTZ
Leadman....KURT HULETT
Buyer/Set Dresser....CHRISTOPHER CARLSON
On Set Dresser....ROBERT BLECKMAN
Set Dressers....MIKE CASEY, FRED PAULSEN, LUIGI MUGAVERO, NICK RAYMOND, MAUREEN OSBORNE
Drapery Foreman....BRAD CURRY
Location Manager....MICHAEL HARO
Assistant Location Managers....ALEX REID, PAUL LUCERO
Casting Assistant....ANYA COLLOFF
Extras Casting....CENTRAL CASTING, TONY HOBBS
Locations Extras Casting/Eureka....CENTRAL COAST PRODUCTION SERVICES, MARILYN MICHEL
Construction Coordinator....JOHN VILLARINO
General Construction Foremen....MIKE VILLARINO, LARRY GUY CLAUSE, JOHN ELLIOTT
Labor Foremen....ANTHONY FEOLA, VLAD PELINOVSCHI
Propmaker Foremen....DONALD HARDENBURG, TOM LIFSEY, ROBERT VANDYKE
Chief Sculptor....FRED ARBEGAST
Plaster Supervisors....DAVE ROBBIE, LOUIS MARQUIS
Paint Supervisor....PATRICK GOMES
Paint Foreperson....NANCY GOMES
Stand-By Painter....TONY LEONARDI
Greens Coordinator....DANNY ONDREJKO
General Foreman....BOB SKEMP
Greens Foremen....JEFFREY BROWN, JEFFREY THOMAS
Stand-By Greens Foreman....KEVIN MANGAN
Greens Standby....RICHARD WILLIAM JONES
Greensmen....CARLO BASAIL, MATT SCHIELTZ, DAVID O'BRIEN, JEFFREY DUKE STEVENS, JOSE OROZCO, LARRY WILLIAMS, TOM SAFRON
Greens Craft Service....RONALD CASTRO
Craft Service....TIM GONZALES, SERGIO TORAL
Display Graphics Supervisor....TODD ARON MARKS
Computer Graphics Design....ALEX MANN
24-Frame Playback/Equipment....STEVE IRWIN
Assistant Editors....PATRICK CRANE, RICHARD BYARD, KEN BLACKWELL
Apprentice Editors....STEVE BAUERFEIND, JULIE ZUNDER
Dialect Coach....NADIA VENESSE
Projectionist....RENE GONZALEZ
Production Controller....JIM TURNER
Production Accountant....STEVIE LAZO
Assistant Production Accountant...KELLY RICHARDS RALSTON
Construction Accountant....KAY JORDAN
Payroll Accountant....EDWARD POVEDA
Assistant Accountant....JAMES T. LINVILLE
2nd Assistant Accountant....SHAUN MCGOVERN
3rd Assistant Accountant....JOSHUA L. T. O'MALLEY
Accounting Assistant....NANCY HONEYCUTT
Post Production Accountant....MARIA DEVANE
Assistant to Mr. Spielberg....CRIS CLARKE
Assistant to Mr. Spielberg....KERI WILSON
Production Assistant to Mr. Spielberg....MARC FUSCO
Assistant to Ms. Kennedy....ELYSE KLAITS
Assistant to Mr. Molen....DIANA TINKLEY
Assistant to Mr. Wilson....LESLIE BARNETT
Assistant to Ms. Curtis....MARK RUSSELL
Assistant to Mr. Koepp....JANICE NAEHU
Key Set Production Assistant....JOHN RILEY
Set Production Assistants....MARC "ROSCOE" ROSKIN, HEATHER SMITH, SEAN RYAN, TODD STONE, LISA ZUSMER
Transportation Coordinator....DENNY CAIRA
Transportation Captains....STEPHEN LUCE, WAYNE WILLIAMS
Transportation Co-Captain....MIKE SHANNON
Picture Car Coordinator....BILL BALLARD
Picture Car Captain....WALLACE FRICK
Picture Car Mechanic....DENNIS MARCHANT
Drivers....JOSE PEDRO ADELMAN, LEO BAKER, KANE BARNETT, JAMES BROWN, TINO CAIRA, ROBERT CAWLEY JR., DENNIS CLARK, TERRY CRNIC, JEFF HATTEN, KELLY JORDAN, LORIN JORDAN, GARY KINCAID, JOHN MORELLO, FRED MOSHIER, ROBERT NEAL, JAMES NORTON, RICH PADGETT, GEORGE POWER, STEVE SORKIN
Transportation Assistant....TRISHA BARNHART
Animal Trainer....JULES SYLVESTER
Studio Teacher....ADRIA LATER
Medical Safety Coordinator....TODD J. ADELMAN
Construction Medic....JUDY MALINOSKI
Assistant Safety Manager/Universal....FRANK M. LITCHAUER
Safety Coordinator/Universal....CHRIS DAYWALT
Stand-Ins....O. B. BABBS, LISA MARIE BOIKO, KATENA GRAHAM, RON SLANINA
Utility Stand-Ins....CRAIG DIFFENDERFER, JAMES C. HOFFMAN
Julianne Moore's Trainer....MICHAEL GEORGE
Aerial Coordinator....ROBERT "BOBBY Z" ZAJONC
Assistant Aerial Coordinator....CHRISTINE BAER
Aerial Unit Director....DAVID B. NOWELL
Camera Aerial Assistant....RICHARD BROOKS BURTON
Twin Star Helicopte....ALAN PURWIN
Blue Hawaiian Helicopters....DAVID CHEVALIER, PATRICIA CHEVALIER
Caterer....RICK BRAININ CATERING
Chef....GERARD R. ARNOULT

Catering Assistants ....ROBERT RAMIREZ, JEFFREY WHITE

Full Motion Dinosaurs and Special Visual Effects by
INDUSTRIAL LIGHT & MAGIC
A Division of Lucas Digital, Ltd.
Marin County, California

Computer Graphics Supervisor........................KEVIN RAFFERTY
CG Sequence Supervisors ....ERIK MATTSON, BEN SNOW
CG Development Supervisor ....EUAN MACDONALD
Lead Digital Character Animators..................DANNY GORDON TAYLOR, DANIEL JEANNETTE, MIGUEL A. FUERTES, DOUG E. SMITH
Associate Effects Supervisor.................................RICK SCHULZE
Digital Character Animators.......GEORGE ALECO-SIMA, CHRIS ARMSTRONG, LINDA M. BEL, PATRICK BONNEAU, DAVID BYERS BROWN, KEN BRYAN, SUE CAMPBELL, BRUCE DAHL, PETER DAULTON, LOU DELLAROSA, MICHAEL EAMES, HAL T. HICKEL, JASON IVIMEY, PAUL KAVANAGH, HEATHER KNIGHT, VICTORIA LIVINGSTONE, JULIE NELSON, DANA O'CONNOR, MARK POWERS, MAGALI RIGAUDIAS, CHI CHUNG TSE, TIM WADDY, BRAD WOODS, WILLIAM R. WRIGHT
Digital Effects Artists ....KEVIN BARNHILL, MICHAEL BAUER, MICHAEL DI COMO, CHRISTINA HILLS, SAMIR HOON, ED KRAMER, TOM MARTINEK, MIN, CURT I. MIYASHIRO, PATRICK NEARY, KENNETH J. NIELSON, KHATSHO JOHN ORFALI, DAVID PARRISH, BRUCE POWELL, AMANDA RONAI-DAHLE, COREY ROSEN, FREDERIC SCHMIDT, B. DURANT SCHOON, JEFF SHANK, DOUG SUTTON, CHRISTOPHER TOWNSEND, JOHN WALKER, ANDY WANG, HOWIE WEED, R. CHRISTOPHER WHITE
Digital Model Supervisor..................................PAUL GIACOPPO
Compositing Supervisors...PABLO HELMAN, JON ALEXANDER
Visual Effects Art Director...................................GEORGE HULL
Lead Viewpainter...SUSAN ROSS
Lead Matchmover...TERRY CHOSTNER
Lead Roto Artist ....JACK MONOGOVAN
Location Matchmover................................JACK "EDSEL" HAYE
Sabre Artists ....CAITLIN CONTENT, GRANT MCGLASHAN
Digital Compositors.................TIM ALEXANDER, JEFF DORAN, MARY MCCULLOCH
Viewpainters.......DONNA ASHLEY BEARD, CATHERINE CRAIG
Visual Effects Editor ....MICHAEL GLEASON
Senior Effects Coordinator ....VICKI L. ENGEL
Visual Effects Coordinators ....CHRISTINE M. OWENS, MEGAN I. CARLSON
Stage Manager ....EDWARD T. HIRSH
Assistant Stage Manager............................DAVID S. DRANITZKE
Effects Director of Photography......................PATRICK TURNER
Model Shop Project Supervisor......................LORNE PETERSON
Matchmove Artists..............SELWYN EDDY III, DAVID HANKS, RANDY JONSSON, JODIE MAIER, DAVID MANOS MORRIS
Rotoscope Artists.....................CHRISTINE CRAM, KATE ELSEN, DEBBIE L. FOUGHT, SUSAN GOLDSMITH, SCOTT CHARLES STEWART, MICHAEL VAN EPS, SUSAN M. WEEKS
Digital Timing Supervisor................................KENNETH SMITH
Digital Matte Artist..PAUL HUSTON
Senior Scanning Operator ....RANDALL K. BEAN
Scanning Operator...MICHAEL ELLIS
CG Resource Assistant...........................KIMBERLY LASHBROOK
Negative Line-Up..ANDREA BIKLIAN
Digital Plate Restoration ....MELISSA MONTERROSA
Assistant Visual Effects Editor ....GREG HYMAN
Projectionist ....KENN MOYNIHAN
Software Development Supervisor................CHRISTIAN ROUET
Software Development........ROD G. BOGART, JIM HOURIHAN, CARY PHILLIPS
Video Engineering ....DANA BARKS
Computer Systems Engineering...........KEN BYER, GREG DUNN
Mechanical Effects...GEOFF HERON
Stage Technicians.................................BILL BARR, DICK DOVA, BOB FINLEY III, MATT HERON, TIM MORGAN
Visual Effects Camera Assistants ....VANCE PIPER
Model Makers—Miniatures Unit ....BARBARA AFFONSO, PHIL BROTHERTON, GIOVANNI DONOVAN, ROBERT EDWARDS, GRANT IMAHARA, IRA KEELER, KEITH LONDON, MICHAEL LYNCH, RODNEY MORGAN, WENDY MORTON, BEN NICHOLS, RANDY OTTENBERG, CHRIS REED, EBEN STROMQUIST, STEVE WALTON
CG Technical Assistants ....MICHAEL CORCOAN, JENNIFER MARY AM NONA, PAUL VEGA
Production Assistants ....MONIQUE GOUGEON, ALICIA MAGNANT
Computer Graphics Staff ....BARRY ARMOUR, KEN MARUYAMA, CLIFF PLUMER
ILM Senior Staff ....PATRICIA BLAU, GAIL CURREY, CHRISSIE ENGLAND, JEFF MANN, JIM MORRIS

Live Action Dinosaurs Designed and Created at
Stan Winston Studio

Effects Supervisors.........JOHN ROSENGRANT, SHANE MAHAN, J. ALAN SCOTT, MARK "CRASH" MCCREERY
Concept Art Director/Designer......MARK "CRASH" MCCREERY
Additional Concept Designers............................JOEY OROSCO, RION VERNON
Hydraulic Design and Supervision ....TIM NORDELLA
Hydraulic Engineer ....LLOYD BALL
Mechanical Designers......RICHARD LANDON, CHRIS COWAN, JON DAWE, BOB MANO, RICH HAUGEN, JEFF EDWARDS, AL SOUSA, KIRK SKODIS
Sevro Control Specialist ....SIMON KATIRAIE
Key Artists ....JOEY OROSCO, GREG FIGIEL, BILL BASSO, CHRIS SWIFT, MARK MAITRE, PAUL MEJIAS, SCOTT STODDARD, DAVE GRASSO, MARK JURINKO, JASON MATTHEWS, JIM CHARMATS, NICK MARRA
Key Technicians..........................JOE READER, TONY MCCRAY, BARRY CRANE
Art Department..................IAN STEVENSON, KEVIN MCTURK, RICHARD DAVISON, LINDSAY MACGOWAN, DAVE MONZINGO, BRUCE SPAULDING FULLER, CHRIS ROBBINS, TRAVOR HENSLEY, RICHIE ALONZO, ROB RAMSDALE, STUART ARTINGSTALL, URSULA WARD, JACQUELINE GONZALES, KEN BRILLIANT, JON NEILL, TIM LARSEN, MIKE SMITHSON, JASON BARNETT, TERRY WOLFINGER
Mold Technical Department......ERIC OSTROFF, JOHN CALPIN, KEITH MARBORY, MIKE HARPER, MICHAEL ORNELAZ, LOU DIAZ, CHRISTIAN LAU, LANCE GILMER, GARY YEE, MARK SISSON, GRADY HOLDER, DARIN BOUYSSOU, DAVE PERTEET, TOM MCLAUGHLIN, MIKE MEASIMER
Mechanical Department....................MATT HEIMLICH, DAVID COVARRUBIAS, BRIAN NEMANNY, JOHN DECKER, MARC IRVIN, LOU GIRARD, PAUL ROMER, JOSH PATTON, KYLE MARTIN
Electronics Department Supervisor....................EMERY BROWN
Electronics Department ....GLENN DERRY, BRUCE STARK, RODERICK KHACHATOORIAN, KUR HERBEL
Fabrication Department Supervisor...................KAREN MASON
Fabrication Department.........BETH HATHAWAY, JUDY BOWERMAN, LYNETTE JOHNSON
Assistants to Stan Winston ....CHUCK ZLOTNICK, KATIE WRIGHT
Production Coordinator.......................................STILES WHITE
Executive in Charge of Operations..TARA MEANEY-CROCITTO
Production Accountant...............................LAURIE TRAMMELL
Courier Coordinator..LYN-DEL FIAGEU

M-Class and Unimog Vehicles Specially Prepared and Provided
Courtesy of Mercedes-Benz

Post Production Executive ....MARTIN COHEN
Post Production Supervisor.............................ERICA FRAUMAN
Re-Recording Mixers ....GARY SUMMERS, GARY RYDSTROM, SHAWN MURPHY
Sound Effects Editors ....KEN FISCHER, TERESA ECKTON, LARRY OATFIELD
Supervising ADR Editor ....MICHAEL SILVERS
ADR Editor ....LINDAKAY BROWN
Dialogue Editors ....SARA BOLDER, EWA SZTOMPKE OATFIELD
Foley Editors ....SANDINA BALIO LAPE, BRUCE LACEY
Assistant Sound Designer ....CHRIS BOYES
Supervising Assistant Editor....................................LISA CHINO
Assistant Sound Editors ....ANDRE FENLEY, CHERYL NARDI, MARCIE ROMANO, MARY WORKS
Foley Artists ....DENNIE THORPE, JANA VANCE
Foley Mixer ....TONY ECKERT
Foley Recordist...FRANK "PEPE" MEREL
Re-Recordists ....RONALD G. ROUMAS, AL NELSON, SCOTT LEVY
Machine Room Operator.....................................DAVE TURNER
Mix Technicians........................GARY A. RIZZO, TONY SERENO
Transfer Supervisor....................................MARNI L. HAMMETT
Digital Transfer........................JONATHAN GREBER, DEE SELBY
Video Services.....CHRISTIAN VON BURKLEO, JOHN TORRIJOS
Music Editor ....KENNETH WANNBERG
Assistant Music Editor.....................KELLY MAHAN JARAMILLO
Music Contractor.......................................SANDY DECRESCENT
Music Preparation...JO ANN KANE
Music Scoring Mixer.......................................SHAWN MURPHY
Scoring Crew............SUSAN MCLEAN, GREG DENNEN, MARK ESHELMAN, PATRICK WEBER, GRANT SCHMITZ, RICHARD DEARMAS
Orchestrations........................JOHN NEUFELD, CONRAD POPE
ADR Mixer..DEAN DRABIN
ADR Recordist..ANN HADSELL
ADR Recorded at ....TODD-AO STUDIOS
ADR Voice Casting..BARBARA HARRIS
Music Recorded at ....SONY PICTURES STUDIOS
Color Timer ....JIM PASSON
Negative Cutter ....GARY BURRITT
Titles and Opticals...PACIFIC TITLE

CONSULTANTS

Museum of the Rockies ....JACK HORNER
Hunter...ROSS SEYFRIED
University of Wisconsin ....TIM EHLINGER

CAST

Ian Malcolm...JEFF GOLDBLUM
Sarah Harding ....JULIANNE MOORE
Roland Tembo ....PETE POSTLETHWAITE
Peter Ludlow ....ARLISS HOWARD
John Hammond ....RICHARD ATTENBOROUGH
Nick Van Owen ....VINCE VAUGHN
Kelly Curtis...VANESSA LEE CHESTER
Dieter Stark..PETER STORMARE
Ajay Sidhu ....HARVEY JASON
Eddie Carr...RICHARD SCHIFF
Dr. Robert Burke..THOMAS F. DUFFY
Tim ....JOSEPH MAZZELLO
Lex ....ARIANA RICHARDS
Carter ....TOMMY ROSALES
Cathy Bowman ....CAMILLA BELLE
Mrs. Bowman ....CYD STRITTMATER
Mr. Bowman..ROBIN SACHS
Senior Board Member ....ELLIOTT GOLDWAG
Board Member...................................J. PATRICK MCCORMACK
Curious Man...ROSS PARTRIDGE
Butler...IAN ABERCROMBIE
Waitress ....SALI LEWALLY
Waiter...MICHAEL CHINYAMURINDI
Workman..DAVID SAWYER
Barge Captain ....GENO SILVA
Barge Captain's Son ....ALEX MIRANDA
Ingen Helicopter Pilot...................ROBERT "BOBBY Z" ZAJONC
Cargo Helicopter Pilots...........BOB BOEHM, BRADLEY JENSEN, ALAN PURWIN, BEN SKORSTAD, RICK WHEELER, KENYON WILLIAMS
Obnoxious Tourist.....................................MICHAEL MILHOAN
Tourist #2...SEAN BARNES

Tourist #3...BRIAN LALLY
Tourist #4 ....KENNY MOSCOW
Tourist #5 ....BRETT HARMAN
Tourist #6..MARK PELLEGRINO
InGen Worker ....GORDON MICHAELS
InGen Worker #1 ....J. SCOTT SHONKA
InGen Worker #2 ....HARRY HUTCHINSON
InGen Guard #1 ....BILL BROWN
InGen Guard #2 ....BRIAN TURK
Harbor Master ....JIM HARLEY
Benjamin...COLTON JAMES
Benjamin's Dad.......................................CAREY EIDEL
Benjamin's Mom......................................KATY BOYER
Unlucky Bastard.....................................DAVID KOEPP
Attorney...EUGENE BASS JR.
Screaming Woman ....BARI BUCKNER
Screamer #1 ....P. B. HUTTON
Screamer #2....................................DAVID ST. JAMES
Screamer #3 ....MARK BRADY
Screamer #4.....................................MARJEAN HOLDEN
Screamer #5 ....JAQUELINE SCHULTZ
Screamer #6 ....DOMINI HOFMANN DE SALGADO
Screamer #7..THOMAS STUART
Ship Driver.................................C. RANSOM WALROD
Police Helicopter Pilot ....DAVID JENE GIBBS
Asian Tourist ....MICHAEL FUJIMOTO
Asian Tourist #2 ....PAUL FUJIMOTO
Asian Tourist #3 ....DARRYL A. IMAI
Asian Tourist #4................................DARRYL OUMI
Screaming Hunter ....VINCENT DEE MILES
CNN Reporter/Himself....................BERNARD SHAW

PUPPETEERS

LLOYD BALL	MARK MAITRE
BILL BASSO	ROBERT NOBORUMANO
EMERY BROWN	KEITH MARBORY
JOHN CALPIN	NICK MARRA
JIM CHARMATZ	KAREN MASON
DAVID COVARRUBIAS	JASON MATTHEWS
CHRIS COWAN	TONY MCCRAY
BARRY CRANE	MARK "CRASH" MCCREERY
RICHARD DAVISON	KEVIN MCTURK
JON DAWE	PAUL MEJIAS
GLENN DERRY	DAVID MONZINGO
JEFF EDWARDS	BRIAN NAMANNY
GREG FIGIEL	TIM NORDELLA
DAVE GRASSO	MICHAEL A. ORNEALZ
BETH HATHAWAY	JOEY OROSCO
RICH HAUGEN	ERIC OSTROFF
MATT HEIMILICH	JOE READER
MARC IRVIN	JOHN ROSENGRANT
LYNETTE JOHNSON	ALAN SCOTT
MARK JURINKO	KIRK SKODIS
RICHARD LANDON	ALFRED SOUSA
LINDSAY MCGOWAN	SCOTT STODDARD
SHANE MAHAN	CHRIS SWIFT

STUNTS

LAURA ALBERT	LES LARSON
PETE ANTICO	DIANE LUPO
SETH ARNETT	TOM LUPO
STANTON BARRETT	RICH MINGA
ROB BOLLINGER	TOM MORGA
TODD BRYANT	HUGH AODH O'BRIEN
DAVID CADIENTE	MANNY PERRY
CHRISTOPHER CASO	CHARLIE PICERNI
DANNY COSTA	CHUCK PICERNI JR.
MIKE DELUNA	STEVE PICERNI
JOHN DEPASQUALE	CHAD RANDALL
CHRIS DURAND	SHAWN ROBINSON
TOM ELLIOTT	TROY ROBINSON
GARY EPPER	CHARLIE ROMANO
JON EPSTEIN	J. P. ROMANO

YURI HINSON	DAVID ROWDEN
TOMMY HUFF	MIKE SCHWELLINGER
KEVIN JACKSON	ADAM SEWELL
CINDA JAMES	MARK STEFANICH
KEII JOHNSTON	BRIAN STEWART
STEVE KELSO	IVAN STEWART
HENRY KINGI	LEE WADDELL
JIM KIRBY	WILLIAM WASHINGTON
JOHN KISHI	ROGER WELLS
SHAWN LANE	ALAN WURTZEL

The Producers Wish to Thank the Following:
JVC
FLEETWOOD RV AND FLEETWOOD ENTERPRISES, INC.
CANYON MOTORCYCLES PROVIDED BY
CAGIVA MOTORS S.P.A.—
VARESE, ITALY
MITSUBISHI ST151 TRANSPORTABLE SATELLITE
TELEPHONES
PROVIDED BY AMSC SKYCELL, INC.
TIMBERLAND
EASTMAN KODAK
USE OF THE CNN WASHINGTON, D.C., BUREAU FOR
FILMING BERNARD SHAW, COURTESY OF CNN. CNN IS A
REGISTERED TRADEMARK OF CABLE NEWS NETWORK, INC.
A TIME WARNER COMPANY. ALL RIGHTS RESERVED.

The Producers Also Wish to Thank the Following:
JERRY SCHMITZ
AMERICAN HUMANE SOCIETY
BEHIND THE SCENES FREIGHT AND TRANSPORTATION
SPECIALISTS
SENATOR TRAVEL—YVES ALBIEZ AND
JENNIFER DEAUGUSTINE
CATHERINE MADIGAN
MURRAY BOYD
JUDITH M. BROWN
CALIFORNIA FILM COMMISSION
HUMBOLDT COUNTY FILM COMMISSIONER—
KATHLEEN GORDON-BURKE
CALIFORNIA STATE PARKS
PATRICK'S POINT STATE PARK
PRAIRIE CREEK REDWOODS STATE PARK
CALIFORNIA STATE RANGERS—BOB ANDERSON AND
KEN ANDERSON
CALIFORNIA CONSERVATION CORPS—DEL NORTE
HAWAII STATE FILM OFFICE
KAUAI FILM COMMISSIONER—JUDY DROSD
THE ISLAND & PEOPLE OF KAUAI
MYLES KAWAKAMI
IRISH BARBER-KANAKAOLE
SAM LEE
AL BURNS
KIPUKAI RANCH:
GENERAL MANAGER—BOBBY FERREIRA
THE RANCH GANG—TYSON FERREIRA, KEKAHJ FERREIRA,
TIPPY AHSAM, SANDRA AHSAM
ILENE LANDRESS, DICK QUINLAN
"SPIN CITY" CREW/NEW YORK
ENTERTAINMENT INDUSTRY DEVELOPMENT
CORPORATION
CITY OF BURBANK
CITY OF ARCADIA
CITY OF PASADENA
COUNTY OF LOS ANGELES ARBORETUM
THE MAYFIELD SENIOR SCHOOL
SOUTHWEST MARINE, INC.
WEST COAST HELICOPTERS
GEO FILM GROUP
CAMERA SUPPORT SYSTEMS
BEAUMONTE CINE SYSTEMS
CHAPMAN/LEONARD STUDIO EQUIPMENT
MUSCO LIGHTS

NIGHT LIGHTS BY BEBEE
REBEL RENTS
TENTING BY AVALANCHE

Filmed at:
Universal City Studios, California
Eureka, California
Kauai, Hawaii
San Diego, California
New York, New York

ORIGINAL SOUNDTRACK ON MCA CDS AND
CASSETTES

THIS FILM MIXED AND RECORDED IN A THX SOUND
SYSTEMS THEATRE

FILMED WITH PANAVISION CAMERAS

Color by DELUXE

DOLBY STEREO
in Selected Theaters

EASTMAN COLOR FILM

THE DIGITAL EXPERIENCE
DTS in Selected Theaters

CERTIFICATE NO.   IATSE
MPAA SEAL   INSIGNIA

A STEVEN SPIELBERG FILM

AMBLIN ENTERTAINMENT

MPAA CODE Classification

Standard Tour Tag